SECI
HEREI

Jill Howard-Jones

Jill Howard-Jones

S.B. Publications

For Ray, who shares my love for Hereford.

First published in 1993 by S.B. Publications
℅ 19 Grove Road, Seaford, East Sussex BN25 1TP.

ISBN: 1 85770 044 9

Typeset, printed and bound by
Manchester Free Press,
Longford Trading Estate,
Thomas Street, Stretford,
Manchester M32 0JT.

CONTENTS

Front cover: St. Ethelbert's tile, Hereford Cathedral
Back cover: Spiral staircase to Cathedral tower
Title page: Crocodile sculpture, Hereford Library and Museum

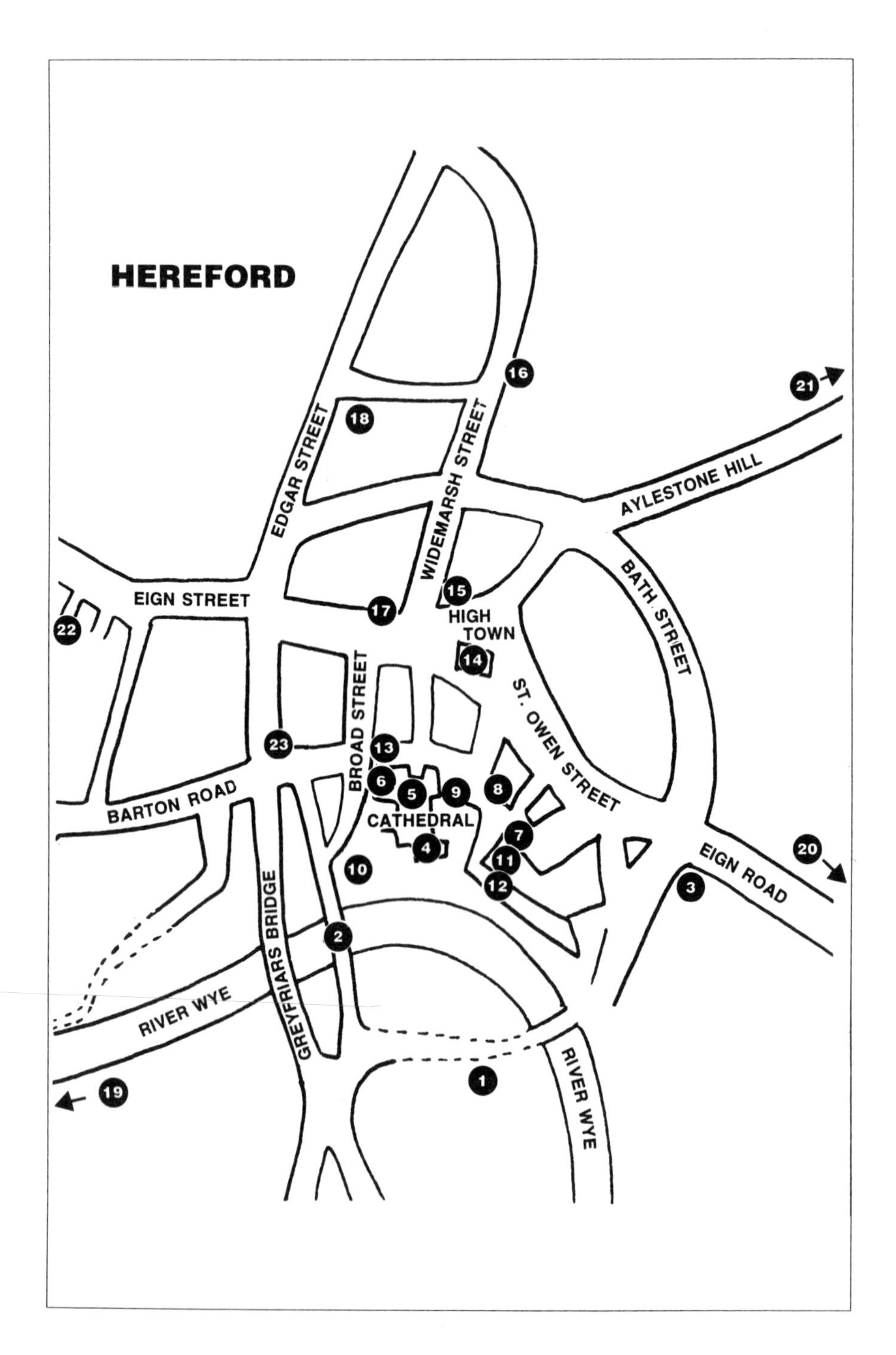
HEREFORD
EDGAR STREET
WIDEMARSH STREET
AYLESTONE HILL
BATH STREET
EIGN STREET
HIGH TOWN
BROAD STREET
ST. OWEN STREET
BARTON ROAD
CATHEDRAL
EIGN ROAD
GREYFRIARS BRIDGE
RIVER WYE
RIVER WYE
1
2
3
4
5
6
7
8
9
10
11
12
13
14
15
16
17
18
19
20
21
22
23

KEY TO MAP

1. Row Ditch, ancient city rampart
2. Old Wye Bridge
3. St.Owen's Court, site of ninth and eleventh century city defences
4. Cloisters of the Vicars Choral
5. Cathedral Tower
6. Great West Door of Cathedral
7. 29 Castle Street, former home of Vicars Choral
8. 1 Castle Street, formerly the Headmaster's House
9. Cathedral Close
10. Bishop's Palace and Terry Waite's Tree
11. Gazebos built to overlook Hereford Castle
12. St.Ethelbert's Well
13. Library, Art Gallery and Museum
14. The Old House
15. Butter Market
16. Coningsby Museum
17. All Saints' Church
18. Cattle Market
19. Water Works Museum
20. Plas Gwyn, Elgar's Hereford Home
21. Brian Hatton Art Gallery
22. Cider Museum
23. Cannon Ball in City Wall

INTRODUCTION

Hereford is like an old friend with a chequered past — a familiar confidant who can be fascinatingly unpredictable, teasingly hugging her secrets to herself but telling just enough to whet my curiosity.

Exploring her is exciting and fun.

This book is not so much a guided tour, but an adventure. There's a sense of achievement when I climb out on to the roof of the Cathedral Tower, when I stoke the ancient boiler at the Water Works Museum and discover a cannon ball in the City Wall.

Each place has its personal story. The secrets of a city are interred in its buildings and the memories of its people — and so it is with Hereford

We can all relate to human fallibility. It's essentially the city's humanity embodied in its history that I've tried to capture: Singing Vicars who couldn't control their tempers, inconsiderate ghost spotters invading the Close, the Bishop who couldn't meet the expenses of his large family, the Artist who seemed to know what horses were thinking, the Chemist who made a tragic mistake and could never forgive himself.

The spirits of Hereford tell her story with gaps that will never be filled. It's been a privilege, however, to share some of her secrets . . . and, above all, it's been fun.

I hope the reader, with the aid of the map references, will also enjoy the secrets Hereford has revealed to me — and find them entertaining.

Jill Howard-Jones

1. Within These Walls
(Map references: l, 2, 3 & 23)

It's no secret that Hereford was a Medieval walled city with six gates and seventeen towers. The Wall was "a good mile", 2250 yards long.

To walk round the City Wall takes little more than an hour — to drive round takes less than ten minutes.

Not a great distance, nor a wide area — yet surprisingly there were 63 inns and 154 alesellers inside Hereford City walls in 1641!

In like spirit, why not start the walk round the City Wall at the Saracen's Head, by the Old Bridge? A large car park is nearby, at the Swimming Pool.

The Old Bridge was once the proud possessor of a City Gate. This Wye Bridge Gate stood on the Saracen's Head side of the river, guarding both bridge and city from the invader. Today, a river bank footpath links the Old Bridge with the New Bridge, built in 1966.

It's after crossing the New Bridge that the City Wall is first seen on the right. The Wall separates long gardens from the car park area beneath the bridge.

Ninth and eleventh century Medieval defences at St. Owen's Court

Of the city's seventeen semi-circular towers, only two remain. The first built at the same time as the defensive wall, is near the traffic lights at the end of the New Bridge. Arrow-slits are still visible, although the tower has lost its former height.

The Wall now disappears into a building, but rises to an impressive height immediately the intersection of the Ring road with St. Nicholas Street has been negotiated. This marks where Friars' Gate once gave the Grey Friars access into the city as their house was outside the walls.

The original City wall is at its best here. Spot the cannon ball, if you can! There's no plaque — nothing to signify its presence, but it's been there since the Civil War, embedded in the wall, about nine feet above the ground.

Now a wide footpath follows the grassy bank between the busy Ring Road and the mighty Wall with its second semi-circular tower.

Eign Gate appears on the right. The Gate is no more but Eign Street has been renamed Eign Gate to commemorate this former entrance into the city. In 1707, folk trod warily here. The Council had uttered a timely warning, trusting "that speedy care be taken at Eygne Gate, the timber being rotten, some stone of considerable weight have fallen down lately to the great astonishment of strangers!"

Eign Gate was the main west gate to Hereford, but like the other five, it was demolished in the eighteenth century, probably in the interests of public safety!

It's left to the Wall to preserve the impression of an enclosed city. City planners have been determined to perpetuate it. Thus Tesco's has a modern reconstruction of the City Wall separating its supermarket from the Ring road, which is itself mainly based on the line of the City ditch.

Admittedly the original wall is less conspicuous now, but it's still worthwhile following the Ring road round to Widemarsh Street. This is where Widemarsh Gate would have stood. A section of the original gatehouse is preserved as a part of the Farmers's Club. In its side wall which faces the road, is a small but prominent wooden door. Carved above the door is "T.C. 1626." T.C. was Thomas Church, Dyer of Cloth. He needed to wash his cloth in the city ditch which passed beneath the drawbridge to Widemarsh Gate. So he added the low door to give him easy access to the ditch. Imagine him doing his washing where traffic lights now control the Ring Road traffic!

The Wall has now gone under the road, but there is no mistaking the Kerry Arms where the Ring road crosses Commercial Street, formerly Bye Street. Bye Street Gate was the largest city gate with the city gaol in its gatehouse.

Seventeenth century low door built to give access to city ditch which formerly passed beneath the draw bridge to Widemarsh Gate

Further along the Ring road, the ancient City wall again stands proud before it dives beneath the Police Station. A cider press with a nineteenth century plaque emphasises the importance of boundaries with "This wall belongs to the land of this side."

As the Wall now disappears for a while, a short cut is recommended through Gaol Street to St. Owen's Street, site of St. Owen's Gate. The City Wall still forms one side of a shop in St. Owen's Street (formerly Townsend's Office Supplies). It then turns sharply left at the end of the garden.

Now is the opportunity to view the only site in England where ninth and eleventh century Medieval defences can be seen together. Go through the archway of St. Owen's Court, which appears private but is in fact a right of way. Beyond the massive six foot wide foundations of the City Wall, Saxon timber defences have been reconstructed.

Turn right out of St. Owen's Court, down Mill Street to the Castle Green, formerly the bailey of Hereford Castle and cross the Victoria Suspension Bridge for a delightful walk across the Bishop's Meadow, and back to the Swimming Pool Car Park.

As it approaches the Car Park, the footpath passes the newly discovered Row Ditch, a neglected city rampart probably dating as far back as Saxon times. This exciting find has now been fenced off to prevent further damage and erosion until it's fully restored. It will then show a section of the city's southbank earthwork. Lined with fearsome metal spikes, it was originally designed to stop enemies establishing a foothold south of the river.

It formed part of the ditch defences protecting the strategic Wye Bridge and other river crossings. More significantly in the long term, it protected Hereford Cathedral from the invader.

A fine view of the Cathedral, and indeed the earthwork that marked its first line of defence can be seen from the Leisure Pool Cafe. Refreshment is welcome for ale-sellers are relatively few these days, and walking round the City Wall is a thirsty business!

Row Ditch, ancient city rampart

Entrance to Hereford Cathedral tower

2. Climb the Cathedral Tower and be Certified!

(Map reference: 5)

You get a certificate signed by the Dean of Hereford if you climb the 218 steps to the top of Hereford Cathedral Tower. It's an unforgettable experience.

Windows shrink and spiral staircase narrows during the climb. Shoes ring on stone worn by those other feet: Royalists peering through slits at Roundheads below, or Roundheads on the lookout for Royalists. Both were here, that's certain.

It's a mighty feat, the central tower, built in the early fourteenth century on the Norman piers of the original squat Norman tower. The existing foundations were levelled up and the new tower built, as we know it today. Its pinnacles decorated with what look like dots from the ground, are in fact the famous ballflowers, universally admired.

Like the icing on the cake, the ballflowers must be saved until last. The spiral staircase brings you first to a door marked 'North Transept'. It appears that you are now in an enormous loft, crossing a wooden bridge over crumbling hills. You're between the ceiling and the roof of the north transept; on the other side of that surging stone lies the magnificent vaulting of the north transept ceiling.

Suddenly you come out onto the gallery where you can look down on the inside of the Cathedral. Against the dark flesh of the oak choir stalls, the choristers' lights look like jewels, sparkling to complement the delicate neck of stone which stretches up behind the High Altar to reach the five-fold Norman arch.

Follow the gallery round and see the Cathedral from four different perspectives. There are the pointed arches in the decorative, geometrical style of Westminster Abbey, rising above the bare tiles of the north transept where St. Thomas Cantilupe's shrine looks so small and lonely. How long the nave, with pews like resting oars! How far away the great west door!

When the gallery tour is completed, it's time to rejoin the spiral staircase. Onwards and upwards to the ringing chamber, where red bell ropes are just asking to be pulled — at your peril! At this point those who don't mind climbing a solid ladder, can go up into the belfry. There in the dim light the monstrous bells weighing as much as forty-five hundred-weight, await the visits of mortals.

Once up there, it's hands over ears if the clock is about to chime the hour! Don't be boomed out before you've spotted 'Gloria Deo In Excelsis'

Completing the climb; a small girl emerges through the door on to the roof

View of Hereford's Old and New Bridges from the top of the Cathedral

engraved on one of the bells! That's the favourite inscription of John Finch, the seventeenth century Hereford bell-founder. There are still over fifty other bells in the county to his credit. When the bell-founding business was slack, Finch turned to brewing to earn some money. He was evidently highly respected, for his burial was actually recorded in a special note at the back of a burial register.

The roof of the belfry is the top of the tower, so the weary may be consoled by the fact that there is only twenty feet to go!

On the last lap the spiral staircase (see back cover) narrows, but before you can feel claustrophobic, welcome daylight spills out from the low door opening on to the roof.

Be warned however, and mind your head as you climb through the narrow doorway!

Welcomed by the freshening wind, you can now enjoy the views. To the north lies Leominster; west is Kingston; east, Ledbury and the Malverns. And what a view to the south! Ancient cloisters square a neat lawn beside the spacious grounds of the Bishop's Palace sweeping down to the Wye.

Don't miss the opportunity of seeing the pinnacles at close quarters. The pinnacle that dared to threaten the south transept has been restored. From the ground it looks like the other three, but close to you can see that it has been completely rebuilt and decorated with new ballflowers.

The new stone is very pink, whereas the original pink sandstone has, over the years, turned grey. Notwithstanding, it's an impressive copy.

The tower is clearly a medieval triumph. In the fourteenth century they chose to copy it by putting another tower at the Cathedral's west end. Unable to provide foundations for it, they used the solid Norman west front to support it, together with the Norman pillars inside and tons of additional masonry. Architecturally it was unprofessional, but it did last for four hundred and fifty years. There was mounting concern about widening cracks but the clergy carried on their services regardless. On Easter Sunday 1786, the Cathedral was packed with worshippers. The following day, when even the Dean and the clergy were absent, the west tower fell down. No injuries were recorded. An Act of God, if ever there was one!

It's reassuring to know, as you descend those 218 steps, that history will not repeat itself! Today the Dean and Chapter put safety first and even give you a certificate for climbing to the top of Hereford Cathedral's Tower!

King's Street from the Cathedral Tower

St. Peter's Church, legendary destination of the Monk ghost

3. Ghost in the Close
(Map reference: 9)

The Cathedral Close is green and tranquil. A vast cushion of immaculate lawn requires the sedate Georgian houses of the Archdeacon and residentiary canons to stand respectfully back from the Cathedral's North Porch. Broad Street curls past the west side of the Close, while on the east side are the former boarding houses of the Cathedral School; red brick School House and Old Deanery, with its private drive and screen of trees.

It's appropriate that peace should reign here for the Close was once a graveyard for the whole city of Hereford. It was compulsory for every citizen to be buried in the Cathedral Close. The Dean and Chapter also insisted that all the funerals should be held in the Cathedral.

In 1362, Roger Side, the Vicar of St. Peter's was actually in trouble for conducting his parishioners' funerals in his own church, before taking their bodies to the Close for committal and burial. The Dean and Chapter were angry at being deprived of their funeral fees! So Roger Side was heavily fined and served a five month prison sentence before his appeal to

From left to right, the houses of the Archdeacon of Hereford, and the Precentor of Hereford Cathedral

the Pope was heard. He was then declared to be legally entitled to take funerals in his own parish church.

The Close, however continued to act as a graveyard for the whole city whose population in the fourteenth century was around 3,000. Prints of the Fall of the West Tower in 1786 show hundreds of tombstones on either side of a railinged path leading from Church Street to the North Porch. The Restoration work that followed included the levelling of the city's burial ground. Surprisingly the attack of "ghost fever" which gripped the Close in the mid 1930s doesn't appear to be related to this ancient burial ground.

A policeman started the ghost craze, when he called out a greeting to what he believed to be a colleague moving across the Close. On hearing him shout, however, the figure vanished, but not before the officer had caught a glimpse of the monk's hood.

Within a week, a local printer had seen the figure in the early hours of the morning. It appeared from behind the Old Deanery, wearing a cassock and cowl, and walking rigidly, with hands at its sides.

A few days later, a resident of Castle Street saw the ghostly monk. The robed figure, its arms folded across its chest, and apparently deep in contemplation, was gliding across the Close.

Monk hunting became the vogue. Large groups of Herefordians kept chilly vigils in the Close and many were rewarded with a glimpse of the monk. One man made it disappear by reciting the Lord's Prayer and the Rosary as he walked towards it.

A woman who fell over in terror, said afterwards, "It frightened me almost to death. It was all so clear, and I am certain it was not a trick of the imagination."

Fascination with the macabre not only gripped the city but also brought ghost spotters from Cardiff on the 2 a.m. train in November. One of the crowd compared the experience to going to a football match. Residents of the Close complained to the police and Cathedral authorities declared that the Close was not haunted. Nevertheless, many alleged sightings of the monk have since occurred.

Who is the monk and why does he haunt the Close? One theory is that he was the Provost of a community of monks. While praying at his altar, he is said to have been murdered by the Welsh.

Hereford was certainly under constant threat from Welsh attack. In 1055, the Welsh with the help of a disgruntled English earl, attacked Hereford. At the West Door of the Cathedral, seven brave canons tried to prevent the enemy entering the Cathedral. They were desperate to protect the building

Hereford Cathedral's Great West Door

which blind Bishop Athelstan had taken forty years to build. The canons were slaughtered on the spot. The Welsh invaders and their allies clambered over their bodies to plunder the Cathedral, before destroying it.

The Norman Cathedral replaced it, the West End being rebuilt again after the Fall of the West Tower in 1786. The Great West Door faces Wales, and takes the full force of the gales that sweep down from the Welsh mountains and turn the Close into the coldest, windswept place in Hereford. Then the stage seems set for a re-enactment of the gruesome murder of the seven canons at the West Door.

Yet they do not haunt the Close. That privilege is the robed monk's, and his alone.

His appearances have also been recorded in St. Peter's Church, where he is apparently heading when he walks across the Close. Some say he's the spirit of St. Peter's Norman founder, Walter de Lacy. Be he Walter or anonymous monk, December seems to have been the most popular month for seeing him!

The New Year banishes December's ghosts. The spirits have fled: only bones remain beneath the Cathedral Close. January 1993 saw hundreds of skeletons dug up by archaeologists working on a special site in the south west corner of the Cathedral precinct, prior to the building of the new Mappa Mundi Museum.

The public were allowed to view these astonishing finds. Down in the trenches hundreds of bones poked out, for many of these graves were dug on top of one another especially in the fourteenth and fifteenth centuries. Local helpers washed the pottery, clay pipes, wine bottles and marbles that might well have belonged to their own ancestors, for this corner of the cemetery was not for the rich and powerful. One girl was buried with her green glass beads on a copper alloy spiral wire. Perhaps her lover bought them for her at the May Fair, which she almost certainly would have attended.

In the Middle Ages, the Fair was always held in the Close. It was known as St. Ethelbert's Fair after the Cathedral's patron saint. The graveyard was then open land, which the Dean and Chapter enclosed in 1389.

To-day the fair is set up in Hereford's main streets, which are closed to traffic for three days. The Big Wheel turns in Broad Street, raising its passengers to the level of the Cathedral roof. The Close, however cannot escape completely from the pulsating, kaleidoscopic beat of the fair, pungent with onions and generator fumes!

After three days, the Fair is gone. The Close is back to its green, tranquil self. In the softness of twilight, tranquillity turns to mystery. Will the monk return to haunt it? That must be his secret!

4. The Singing Vicars
(Map references: 4 & 7)

The passage to the College Cloisters is opposite Hereford Cathedral's south east door. This medieval corridor turns sharply to the left, leading the visitor beneath a fan vaulted porch, into a picturesque quadrangle with a garden in its midst. It's a scene that's remained virtually unchanged for 500 years. Here the 28 Vicars Choral lived in separate dwellings. One of their houses is now open to the public.

The Vicars Choral were so called because they were priests required to sing the daily services in the Cathedral during the late Middle Ages. At first there was a problem over their accommodation. Unlike monks they were not legally entitled to own the equivalent of a monastery. Richard II solved this problem by giving them the status of a College for 28 singing priests, with its own seal and the right to hold property.

Their College was situated on the south side of Castle Street and now forms part of the Cathedral School. The original roof timbers under the eaves are still visible in No 29 Castle Street in the upstairs flat, which now provides attractive accommodation for teaching staff.

Entrance to the Vicars Choral Cloister

It wasn't, however, ideal for the Vicars Choral. They had to attend seven daily services. That meant negotiating the unlit muddy path to the Cathedral where hooligans lay in wait. Storms and darkness could also turn that short walk into an endurance test. Fortunately the Vicars Choral had two good friends: Earl Ferrers and Bishop Stanbury. The Earl who lived opposite at the junction of Ferrers Street and Castle Street was their benefactor. The Bishop gave up part of his palace garden to build the College of Vicars Choral on the south side of the Cathedral itself, complete with quadrangle, gateway and cloister.

This was all built within three years, between 1472 and 1475. How grateful they must have been to be able to walk, safe from muggers and the inclement weather, along a corridor connecting their quad with the Cathedral!

The Cloisters also provided each Vicar Choral with his own house. Under the original arrangements, this had one room upstairs and one down, with fireplaces for log fires. The house now open to the public has a typical walled garden, dwarfed by the Cathedral which gives the illusion of sprouting from the garden wall! An upstairs window also provides an attractive view of the garden of the adjoining Bishop's Palace.

An idyllic setting in the daytime, but imagine the Vicar leaving his home in the dark, flickering lights from cresset torches casting eerie shadows on stone walls as he tramped along the cobbled cloister to take part in his seventh service of the day.

A shorter walk would have taken him to dinner in the refectory, now the lofty College Hall where portraits of past Vicars gaze benignly from the walls.

The College of the Vicars Choral was a self-contained community and subject to discipline. They were not allowed "to wander abroad from the ringing of bell for Vespers until after Compline", unless it was necessary to cross the churchyard (now the Close), before setting off on, or returning from a long journey. They were prohibited from frequenting taverns or dishonourable places or from wandering round the city streets at night.

"Decent apparel" was the order of the day. They were required to cover their heads with a tippet when going into town, and they also had to be accompanied by a servant.

An incident during the Civil War indicates the rigid observance of this rule. The Roundheads turned the Vicars out of the College, which was used as lodging for the homeless. One Vicar lost his hat to the Parliamentary soldiers, so borrowed a bonnet from a female servant every time he ventured out!

The Vicars Choral Cloister

The concern of the Dean and Chapter over the behaviour of the Vicars Choral is thought to be reflected in the extraordinary elaborate carvings on the high rafters and beams of the Cloisters' oak roof. Look upwards as you walk back to the Cathedral along the final stretch of the Cloister! There you will see a wolf with menacing teeth threatening a woman's buttock, a pelican feeding its young with its blood, a nun wearing only a head veil and carrying a comb and a sow displayed with saddle and stirrups. These carvings represented warnings against licentious behaviour — which the medieval congregations would certainly have recognised!

Records indicate that such warnings didn't have a lasting effect! In 1598, for instance, a Vicar not only uttered indecent words but threw a knife at another Vicar during dinner! The previous year he hit a servant in the Buttery with a key. In 1601 one Vicar was in trouble for assaulting another in The Cloister "to ye effusion of blood", while another had entertained a woman in his chamber from "the hour of one o'clock in the afternoon on December 1 to the hour of seven o'clock on the morrow, being the 2nd of December"!

One of their last recorded misdemeanours was participation in smoking concerts at the Green Dragon in 1885. After that, they were predictably forbidden to appear at any establishment where intoxicating liquors were sold.

Nevertheless, the contribution of the Vicars Choral to the musical tradition of the Cathedral must not be underestimated. To-day that tradition is maintained by the Cathedral Choir whose daily singing of Evensong at 5.30 p.m. is not to be missed.

Neither must Bishop Stanbury, friend of the Vicars Choral be forgotten. His memorial is the exquisite tiny chantry chapel on the north side of the Cathedral. Here is a magnificent example of fan vaulting in a thin-panelled ceiling of delicately ribbed stone, probably the work of the same mason responsible for the fan-vaulted porch of the Cloister.

The stained glass windows picture scenes from Bishop Stanbury's life. One portrays him crossing the Old Bridge on his way to his enthronement in the Cathedral, shown here with its original west tower. He is, of course, accompanied by his choir: the inestimable Vicars Choral!

It's fitting, therefore, that a trip to the Cloisters which he built for the Vicars Choral, should end here — in the Stanbury Chantry Chapel!

Hereford Cathedral showing the entrance to the Cloisters

Carved re-enactment of Dean Croft's heroic stand against the Roundheads

5. Dean Croft Preaches to Broad Street

(Map reference: 6)

Approached from King's Street or the end of Broad Street, the West Front of the Cathedral looks very imposing . . . so imposing that it is easy to miss the carved re-enactment of Dean Croft's heroic stand against the Roundhead musketeers who were about to gun him down.

He is standing in his famous wooden pulpit. This remains inside the Cathedral usually by the St. John's door but being conveniently portable, its location can vary. However a glance at the pulpit carved on the West Front will guarantee its instant recognition. Imagine a large panelled wooden box on legs with a door opening on to three wooden steps.

From that pulpit Herbert Croft preached his dramatic sermon after witnessing the Roundhead soldiers vandalising and looting his Cathedral. It's said they hacked at the apostles carved round the Norman font. They defaced other monuments, stole old candlesticks and damaged brasses and stained glass windows. During the ensuing service which the Dean insisted on taking as normal, he used his sermon to boldly and sharply condemn their sacrilege. At this, the officers in the congregation began to mutter angrily among themselves prompting the musketeers to prepare their guns. They levelled them at the Dean waiting for the command to fire. The brave Dean's life was only saved by the timely intervention of the chivalrous Roundhead Commander, Colonel Birch.

Shortly afterwards, Dean Croft was driven out with the other Cathedral clergy and not allowed back until the Restoration.

Within days of his return to the Deanery on Boxing Day 1661, he was made Bishop of Hereford by Charles II and required to move into the Bishop's Palace.

In the New Year, it was recorded that "the Bishop hath won the hearts of all sorts of people", confirming "at least 500 persons" and almost certainly addressing them from the "Croft" pulpit where he had denounced the sacrilegious soldiers.

His thirty years as Bishop marked him as a compassionate man. Every week he distributed dole at the Palace Gate to sixty poor people.

Of course he wasn't popular with everyone! He was displeased with clergy who weren't living in their parishes, but at the same time he understood their plight. Absentee priests needed to draw income from other benefices, yet they were aware of their own inadequacy and poor training. Their congregations drawn from lonely hamlets and scattered hill farms were suspicious of strangers, but invariably loyal to the priest who

The Croft Pulpit

lived amongst them. All this Bishop Croft saw and wrote down for the King to read. By the time of his death at the age of 88, there were no absentee canons and fewer poor clergy.

He is buried beneath the Bishop's Throne but his black marble monumental slab is in the South Transept. Between 1848 and 1852, certain slabs were moved and not replaced in their original positions. Herbert Croft's was one but he remains buried by his old friend Dean Benson as his slab's inscription "in vita conjuncti, in morte non divisi" implies.

Samuel Pepys recalls Herbert Croft as "an old good man" who "made an excellent sermon" in London on March 17th, 1667. It certainly can't have excelled the sermon he persists in giving from his wooden pulpit on the West Front of Hereford Cathedral!

Entrance to the Cloisters, Hereford Cathedral

Tudor gatehouse leading to the Bishop's Palace

6. The Bishop's Great Hall and Terry Waite's Tree

(Map reference: I0)

Through the black and white Tudor gatehouse with the massive wooden door at the end of Hereford's Broad Street is the Bishop's Palace. Unlike many ancient episcopal palaces, it has remained the Bishop's home through the centuries. Georgian brick mingles with Victorian in its attempt to meet the individual needs and tastes of Bishop after Bishop.

To-day you are likely to find the Bishop at home. That certainly didn't apply in the Middle Ages. Travel was both difficult and dangerous so the Bishop frequently stayed at one of his twenty-four episcopal manors scattered over his extensive diocese.

His household too, would have been about ten times larger than that of our present Bishop. Medieval bachelor bishops lived in princely style. Their households included squires, serving-men, lesser servants and over a dozen pages. There were cooks, a falconer, a farrier, palfreyman, butler, gatehouse keeper, a warden for his private prison and even a champion at arms to fight any duels! And this enormous staff served a single Bishop with no family to support!

Remains of the ancient giant sycamore beside its replacement, planted by the famous hostage's friend in gratitude for Terry Waite's release

Henry VIII changed this pattern when he broke away from the Roman Catholic Church. Married bishops began to move into the Bishop's Palace, with their wives and children.

In 1635 Theophilus Field who had six children to support was made Bishop of Hereford. One of his descendants, Mary Ann Wolfe (nee Field) recently made a pilgrimage from Miami to Hereford. The lot of her illustrious ancestor was clearly not a happy one! "The poor man was always in debt," Mary Ann revealed, "so he implored his benefactor, the Duke of Buckingham to get him a bishopric. He had his eye on the rich diocese of Hereford but he had to wait seven years before the see became vacant. When he eventually became Bishop of Hereford, the shock was too great and he died, after only six months, leaving his six children fatherless." The effect on Mary Ann? She's now Chairman of Planned Parenthood in Miami!

Large families like that of Theophilus had to be accommodated so the Palace needed more bedrooms. Bishops' wives also required more privacy and comfort than offered by the medieval structure of the Palace based on an open hall. So at the beginning of the eighteenth century, the Great Hall was re-modelled and divided into five compartments. The new Hall which forms the basis of the present one, stretches across the building rather than along it, as the original Norman hall did. Its front door opens on to the cobbled courtyard and its opposite number onto the spacious Palace gardens sloping down to the Wye.

The fact that to-day the Great Hall is probably the most distinctive room in Hereford is mainly due to John Eastaugh. He became Bishop in 1974, almost 1300 years after Bishop Putta, thought to have been Hereford's first Bishop in 676. The Great Hall was therefore restored by Bishop Eastaugh as part of the 13th hundred anniversary celebrations.

Rarely have chandeliers and episcopal portraits hung in such a fresh and sunny place where yellow, white and gold are the predominant colours.

Bishop Eastaugh and his successor Bishop John Oliver have allowed its regular use for numerous recitals. The cultural role of the Palace in the life of Hereford has thus been re-established, in an elegant but essentially domestic setting. Even the Bishop's cats have been known to join in recitals, making a notable and amusing contribution to the Cats' Chorus!

The many functions held in the Great Hall make it readily accessible to visitors. The rest of the Palace is obviously private, but the Palace Library has provided some fascinating reading for local historians. The changing role of the Bishop himself has effected the structure of his palace. In the Middle Ages, Bishops of Hereford represented both Church and State in their working life. The occupant of the Palace could be a Lord Chancellor or Treasurer of England as well as a Bishop. As Bishops became less involved with affairs of state, the Palace became a centre for the administration of the diocese. By the seventeenth century, the Bishop's study was assuming greater importance. To-day the Bishop's study has offices adjoining for administrative and secretarial staff.

These offices, like the Great Hall look out on the courtyard which surrounds a lawn where hundreds of crocuses bloom in the spring. Above them stood a giant sycamore that had been part of the Bishop's garden for centuries. Its existence could be traced back to 1600.

In 1991 Roy Finch, the tree surgeon from Malvern who had care of all the Palace trees, pronounced it unsafe. Because of its historical link with the Palace, it was not cut down but pollarded for safety and carefully conserved. About ten foot of trunk remains and from that new growth is sprouting.

Nevertheless it would never aspire to its former glory, so a new tree was needed to replace it. The planting of its successor, a rare sycamore, coincided with the release of hostage Terry Waite. So on December 5th 1991, a local priest, the Reverend Barry Irons from Breinton who had

Bishop's Palace and Cathedral from the River Wye

been best man at Terry's wedding, planted the new sycamore when it had been dedicated by the Bishop, in gratitude for his friend's release.

Thus the two trees, symbols of the continuity of bishopric and diocese through the ages are seen by the many visitors coming in and out of the Great Hall at the Bishop's Palace.

7. Gazebos that once Viewed Hereford Castle
(Map reference: 11)

Two gazebos overlook Redcliffe Gardens. These garden pavilions sited to command a view, or more simply "gazing abodes", are conveniently close to the Cathedral. After leaving the Close by the Castle Street entrance, turn right down Quay Street, which formerly led to a cobbled quay for barges and you'll see the gazebos on the left, rising with dignity to assert their claim to the view.

The view is pleasant but hardly remarkable. So why the gazebos?

The answer is that they were built to command a view of Hereford Castle. It would certainly have still been a view worth seeing in the seventeenth century with its tall keep on a high mound.

In the early sixteenth century however, Hereford Castle was already doomed. Leland wrote that it "tendeth towards ruin", despite walls which were "highe and stronge and full of great towers".

The moat would have passed in front of the gazebos, continuing round to the Castle Pool, the only section still in existence. Having a drink in the

Gazebo originally built to command a view of Hereford Castle, now incorporated into a cottage, with Hereford Cathedral in the background

The two gazebos from Castle Hill. Note their elevated position which originally gave them a good view of the Castle

Castle Pool Hotel Gardens is a good way to see the remains of the moat, attractively complemented by bird life and mature shrubs.

For the Castle you need more imagination! But the monument leaves you in no doubt. "On this site stood the Norman Keep of Hereford Castle circa 1070."

In the twelfth century it was a royal stronghold with a bailey which eventually enclosed the whole of Castle Green. On what is now landscaped as a open park area, once stood a mighty castle with ten towers and a large keep, built to withstand Welsh invasion. The bailey contained the King's great hall, the county hall, private chambers for the King and Queen and their knights, chapel, treasury, stable, two gaols, a building for seige engines and various offices including a kitchen, mill and bakery. Records tell us how the King's Chamber was whitewashed and wainscoted in 1245, while the Queen's Chamber was lengthened, wainscoted, painted and provided with a wardrobe, fireplace and latrine.

Follow the tarmac paths round the bailey in exceptionally dry weather, and it's possible to see the regular parched marks showing where the stone buildings of the Castle once were. When they were demolished in the late seventeenth and eighteenth centuries, their foundations were left in the ground.

Here lie the stones that held Henry III and Prince Edward prisoners in Hereford Castle during the Baron's War in 1265. They were imprisoned because Hereford supported Simon de Montfort in his baronial opposition to Henry III's misrule. Prince Edward was allowed to ride outside the castle walls in a friendly race with his guards. However he soon tired out his guards' mounts and escaped on a fast steed which the Earl of Gloucester had sent him for that purpose!

In the fourteenth century, the Castle was still impressively fortified. It had to accommodate English men-at-arms to cope with Owen Glendower's onslaught on the three valleys of the rivers Dee, Severn and Wye. English King after English King arrived to tussle with the Welsh. But when the Welsh had been defeated once and for all, its upkeep was neglected.

It suffered considerable damage during the Civil War, but does not seemed to have played a significant part during the sieges and occupations of the city.

The Governor's Lodge, however still stands, its original beams blackened from fire during the Civil War. A plaque marks it as "Castle Cliffe, mediaeval water-gate of Hereford Castle, Governor's Lodge and later the Bridewell." It's now a private house but during its life as the Bridewell, which ended in 1880 when it was sold for £500, it served as a prison for unruly apprentices.

Where apprentices were disorderly and bloody battles were waged is now a bandstand . . . and an ornamental pool! The tranquillity at least allows time for thoughts of those former scenes to drift into the consciousness.

And the gazebos remain! One has been incorporated into a cottage, the other is used by the maintenance staff of Hereford Cathedral School. No longer do they peer over the moat, at the remains of a royal fortress. Instead they nonchalantly lift their gaze from the private rose gardens at their feet to the secluded Redcliffe Gardens beyond.

On reflection it's more than a pleasant view: the past has lent enchantment to it.

All Saints' Church from Broad Street, during the early stages of work on the spire

8. The Church with the Crooked Spire
(Map Reference: 17)

All Saints' is an extraordinary church. It has no churchyard, nor lychgate; it stands literally on the pavement of Hereford's shopping precinct, wedged between Boots the Chemist and Burtons' Menswear.

Its early history is a secret, lost in the mists of time. What has been established though, is that seven hundred years ago, the first All Saints' stood here, by the North Gate of the Saxon City. A part of that first church has been rediscovered.

At the Chancel entrance, a hole in the floor reveals the fine clustered pier at the base of a pillar, under an exposed arch. If this ornate column exemplifies the original architecture of the Church, it was rich indeed.

Why then was the original church not completed? Perhaps the foundations were weak, for this part of Hereford was formerly a swamp. Or was All Saints' another casualty of Welsh aggression?

Rebuilding seems to have spanned two hundred years. Numerous alterations and enlargements were introduced, most notably the spire with its gabled openings, which was added in the fourteenth century.

The imposing spire is a famous Hereford landmark. It dwarfs the Cathedral. Not only does it rise to 240 feet, the equivalent of a twenty-storey tower block, it is also bent . . . but not as bent as it used to be!

The famous kink has caused considerable comment over the centuries, not least among apprehensive citizens who have gazed upwards and wondered if the whole lot was going to come down on their heads! It was a realistic concern. Something had to be done.

Various schemes were launched to meet the cost of the urgent repairs. One involved letting the recess between the Church and Boots to a street trader. His flower stall immediately became a catalyst for controversy. Local florists objected and so did another flower seller who for years had traded, a few yards away by the church wall. Some even said the new site would put pedestrians at risk, because they would be forced to walk round buckets of flowers, protruding on to the High Street pavement.

Finally it was agreed that the new stall could stay, provided it didn't obstruct the footpath. After all, the Council admitted it did add brightness, colour and activity to an "otherwise unused" area. The original flower seller also continued to trade. A flower market was flourishing in the shadow of the ancient church!

Meanwhile work on the bent spire had begun. Seeing it shrouded in four miles of scaffolding, an observer remarked that it looked like a giant

All Saints' Church after the crooked top of the spire had been removed

Flower stall in the recess between All Saints' Church and Boots

Christmas tree. So in December 1992, the idea was taken up; coloured lights adorned the scaffolding. An enormous multi-coloured rocket appeared to defy the force of gravity, as it hung suspended against the night sky.

Unfortunately some unidentified daredevils saw this as a invitation to climb the scaffolding at night. They left their litter 240 feet up for the steeplejacks to find. This alarming discovery prompted the Vicar to warn the public of the great danger involved in climbing the spire unsupervised by steeplejacks.

The work of straightening the spire was nearing its close. The kink was gradually reduced. The two foot curve originally created by Medieval engineers and made worse by Victorian restoration work was now a mere eight inches off centre. The regilded weather cock when replaced, probably never noticed the difference!

It's consoling, perhaps to know that the spire can never totally lose its unique kink. It can never be totally straight because the tower itself isn't straight.

All Saints' is, and always will be Hereford's church with the crooked spire. That kink, albeit reduced, is an important part of its heritage.

9. The St. Ethelbert Trail
(Map reference: 12)

A Prince Charming from East Anglia brutally murdered in Hereford on May 20th 794 A.D. is Hereford Cathedral's patron saint.

Why was he murdered? And what did he do to deserve the title of 'saint'?

The story begins in King Offa's Palace, thought to have been at Sutton Walls, four miles from Hereford. Offa of Mercia was strong, powerful and very ambitious. He had coins minted giving him the title of King of all England.

Ethelbert had just succeeded to the throne of East Anglia. Cunningly, Offa offered his youngest daughter, Elfrida to the eligible bachelor as a bride. Thereby, he clearly hoped to have virtual control over Ethelbert's kingdom.

Offa, however had problems with his own wife, the fair Quendrida. A translation from the medieval Latin of the Hereford Breviary found in the Cathedral Library records how 'The Queen seeing Ethelbert's beauty was violently enamoured, and could not control her desires. She revealed her shameful thoughts by the expression of her eyes . . . The chaste youth fearing God, abhored so great a wickedness and fled from her."

Enraged, she told Offa, so the story goes, that Ethelbert planned to seize Offa's kingdom. Offa didn't believe her at first, but once under the influence of strong drink, he admitted that he wanted Ethelbert killed — provided he wasn't personally responsible for the murder.

The Queen replied. "Thy sword shall harm him not, O King", and put the matter into the hands of Gymbert, the warder of Offa's castle.

The murder scene is depicted on a large tile in the Cathedral chancel floor, which gives the date as 793. The assassin stands with sword uplifted, ready to strike off the head of Ethelbert. The sword was according to the Breviary, Ethelbert's own, implying that he was actually killed in his sleep.

The body and severed head of the murdered king were carried away in a waiting cart by Gymbert and his men. They drove down the hill from Offa's castle intending to throw the corpse into the River Lugg. Then they remembered the Queen's command that it should be buried, so they buried the body and head beside the river, and fled to a safe hiding place.

Offa's remorse was great. He reacted by imprisoning the queen and trying desperately to make his peace with God. The Archbishop used the opportunity to demand "much almsgiving". Thus Offa undertook to replace the "small mean" church in Fernlega (Hereford) with "a goodly

The site of St. Ethelbert's Well, with the stone effigy of St. Ethelbert above a drinking fountain, Castle Hill, Hereford

church of stone and endow the same with large possessions so that mass shall be sung continually for the soul of the young king" . . . and so Hereford Cathedral was built.

The St. Ethelbert's Trail spans the time lapse between his murder and the recovery of his body for burial.

King Offa commanded that it should be found but it seemed an impossible task for Gymbert and his followers had fled. Exhausted by the fruitless search, the king's men came to a place called Marden beside the River Lugg. Suddenly a bright light and spring of water appeared close to the river. There they found the holy body wrapped in a mean cloak, with the severed head.

Borrowing a cart from a nearby farm,they placed the corpse in it and set out for Hereford. Then one of them, straining his eyes in the extreme darkness of that night, yelled out that the head had gone!

He jumped down and rushed off into the darkness to look for the missing head. The others waited anxiously. Meanwhile their friend on his macabre mission, heard someone singing and shouting for joy.

The singer turned out to be the former blind man of Marden who had stumbled on something on the road and had immediately and miraculously

St.Ethelbert's murder depicted on a large tile in the chancel of Hereford Cathedral (see also front cover)

Fourteenth century statue of St. Ethelbert standing by the High Altar in the Cathedral

received his sight. This was the first miracle associated with the head of the Martyr Ethelbert and it's said to have happened on Aylestone Hill in Hereford.

So let's follow the head of St.Ethelbert down Aylestone Hill on its journey from the hallowed source of Ethelbert's Spring at Marden to the Cathedral where many healing miracles subsequently occurred.

As we turn into Castle Street, notice St. Ethelbert's Hospital founded in 1225. These picturesque almshouses with beautiful gardens reaching to the remainder of the Castle Moat were originally a home for ten poor old people. By 1805, they housed ten old ladies who were required to attend morning and evening service in the Cathedral. They had their own pew and were obliged to wear a simple uniform of a short cape and a cap. On Sundays they were given a penny, besides receiving a daily loaf of bread. Today the six houses are converted into modern self-contained apartments. The residents are women of exceptional character who have served the church, in keeping with St. Ethelbert's shining reputation. Instead of the Sunday penny, they receive a token 75p at Christmas.

Instead of continuing your walk down Castle Street, let the St. Ethelbert's Trail lead you down the sign-posted path to the Castle Green, to enjoy the gardens of his almshouses. Then turn right along the path that follows the backs of the houses in Castle Street.

You will find yourself in Castle Hill and there in the wall is a stone head effigy of St. Ethelbert above a drinking fountain. The water flows erratically and few today realise that this well of St. Ethelbert was formerly revered for its miraculous powers. The saint's head is said to have passed this spot and probably rested here on its final journey.

So on went that precious head to the Cathedral chancel . . . where the trail must end. Standing on the tile that commemorates his murder, don't miss the fourteenth-century statue of St. Ethelbert standing in the sanctuary.

Still wondering what Ethelbert did to deserve recognition as a saint, apart from getting himself murdered? Perhaps the hymn sung at the annual service on St. Ethelbert's Day (May 20th), provides the answer:

He repelled with detestation
All the queen's solicitation,
Who enraged at charms despised
Presently his death devised;
Blest his lot thus to lay down
An earthly for a heavenly crown.

Hereford Cathedral School: No.1 Castle Street formerly the Headmaster's House, now classrooms

The author's classroom, formerly the Headmaster's Drawing Room

10. Revelations from the Headmaster's Drawing Room
(Map reference: 8)

Tradition claims Putta as the first Bishop of Hereford in 676. Bede adds that "Putta served God and taught music where desired."

Therefore, choirboys, whether they desired it or not, were probably singing in a cathedral in Hereford in the Dark Ages — certainly in the Middle Ages.

To provide for their education, the Cathedral School was established. Discipline was strict. In 1384 Bishop Gilbert appointed Richardus de Cornwaille as Headmaster to govern the boys "with birch and rod." Their faults were punished no doubt according to St. Benedict's rule "by rigorous fasting or corrected by sharp stripes."

A century later, a boy would no doubt have also been punished by his peers for daring to wear a red rose in support of the House of Lancaster during the Wars of the Roses. Locally the powerful Mortimers were known to favour the House of York.

During the Civil War, pupils would have been staunch Royalists. After all, Charles I was their revered benefactor and he is still remembered with gratitude at the School's annual Commemoration Service. His execution in 1649 must have been traumatic for staff and pupils alike.

During the Commonwealth, school life would have been disrupted, when the desolate Cathedral had its monuments mutilated and its clergy ousted from their stalls.

One famous pupil of this period was the poet, Thomas Traherne. He was evidently educated as a staunch Protestant, according to the violent sermons he preached against the Church of Rome. He left for Brasenose College, Oxford, in 1652, forging links between his school and his college which have survived to this day.

Fortunes of School and Cathedral improved with the Restoration of Charles II. Choristers, however, might not have seen it that way! A seventeenth-century document describes their "leisure hours".

"As often as they can be spared from the Church and Singing school, they shall be taught the Grammar, or if they be not capable thereof, to write very well, or to cast accounts or to play upon the virginal or harp, or in some other liberal sciences become an honest man."

Today the chorister's life is still a hard one. He spends eighteen hours a week over and above a full daily routine in the Cathedral school, rehearsing and singing. He is also required to learn an instrument. Prep and games have to be squeezed in, not forgetting visits to the Buttery, the School

Tuck Shop, a delightfully restored timbered building in Quay Street.

It is hard work, but he discovers that his voice is appreciated; he is part of the great choral tradition of Hereford Cathedral. In his boarding house, he is respected — for he is a chorister.

The boarders originally only occupied School House, an imposing red-brick building facing the Cathedral's Bishop's Cloister and backing on to School Yard where boys once played fives, and staff now park their cars. In 1918 the Headmaster, anticipating a decline in day boys due to competition from the new Hereford Secondary School, decided that he must make room for more boarders.

So he bought No. 1 Castle Street. This provided him with a new house, and, at the same time, could be adapted to the needs of a second house for boarders. Thus, although boarders had previously comprised only about a third of the school, by 1919 they were outnumbering day boys by about three to one.

No. 1 Castle Street looks much the same today although it stands next to the new Portman Technology Centre, completed in December 1992.

Behind the blue door of No. 1, historic photographs of choir and school are constant reminders of the past in the spacious square hall. A pupil's diary for 1917 is among the treasures displayed under glass.

School House, Hereford Cathedral School

The Buttery, Quay Street, the attractive School Tuck Shop

A strong smell of coffee issues from the Monitors' Common Room on the left, once the Headmaster's Study. Now important selected Sixth formers rush in and out in their black gowns. The door on the far right of the hall leads to the kitchens, and the one on the far left to another, smaller hall in the shadow of a Jacobean oak staircase. Across this hall is the door to what was once the Headmaster's Drawing room, with its impressive bay window overlooking the garden.

When I joined the teaching staff in 1973, the Headmaster's drawing room had become the Masters' Common Room and for the past sixteen years, it has been my classroom.

It is spacious, even with its twenty-eight desks all occupied. Of course, the room, for me, is full of memories. The obstinate stain on the ceiling confounding the most diligent decorator is a memento of the late Bishop's youngest son. One memorable night he left his bath running — and flooded us out below!

My past, however, is only a fraction of this room's history. The place has a sense of dignified outrage; the marble mantelpiece accepts the hardboard wedged in its fireplace with a bad grace, as though it remembers, as some of my colleagues do, what it was like when Mr. Peebles was Headmaster here from 1957–67.

They attended parties here, passing pretty maids in the hall way bustling to and fro with the silver as they were ushered into the drawing room. The Headmaster would be standing in front of the great log fire, his powerful frame almost concealing it. He would tweak his braces in welcome, while his son played Listz on the grand piano. After a sumptuous dinner, the men would withdraw for their port, leaving their wives to converse with the Head's wife. This was an experience which, I gather, the wives didn't relish!

Hereford Cathedral School was a man's world alright! One young master's wife, a qualified teacher in her own right, was brought in to do some teaching because a master was ill. She was told to take her coffee with the Secretary — women didn't go into the Common Room! Admittedly the school was much smaller in those days. The morning service was held in the Lady Chapel, whereas today staff and pupils fill the whole Cathedral.

When I arrived in 1973, the school was still a male bastion. I was one of the first three women teachers employed to coincide with the first intake of girls. Gradually the place has become more civilized! For instance the brutal tradition of "ducking" new pupils has disappeared or, at any rate, dwindled into tokenism.

Boarding is being phased out to accommodate the increasing numbers of day pupils, for whom travelling to school from remote villages no longer seems a problem. In September 1993 No. 1 Castle Street ceased to be a boarding house, and the dormitory above my room has become another classroom.

Hereford Cathedral School continues to adapt to the times, but its tradition as an ancient choir school remains.

The connection between School and Cathedral is symbolised in the person of the Boy Bishop.

Every December, a pupil who is an ex-chorister is chosen by the Choir Master and Cathedral Chapter to be Boy Bishop. His appointment goes back to medieval times when Bishops were proud powerful statesmen. During the annual special ceremony in Hereford Cathedral in early December, the Boy Bishop sits on the Bishop's throne while the Bishop takes a lower seat to signify "putting down the mighty from their seat" and "exalting the humble and meek." Ex-Boy Bishops always tell me that the most demanding part of the service is preaching the sermon, but their training as choristers stands them in good stead.

No doubt Hereford's first Bishop who allegedly "served God" and "taught music" back in the seventh century would have thoroughly approved.

11. High Spirit in High Town
(Map references: 14 & 15.)

High Town, site of Hereford's ancient Norman market place, is where it all happens — from Morris dancing to protest marches. Every day is different; a stall promoting a cause is replaced by a balloon seller, buskers have given way to a mobile exhibition. This is where the Bishop ceremonially receives his annual rent for the May Fair: the traditional 12½ bushels of wheat. Only the pigeons remain constant, feasting on considerate crumbs from pastries purchased from the Cathedral Bakery just inside the Butter Market, to satisfy shoppers resting on the seats in the square.

The nineteenth century Butter Market complete with clock tower, houses stalls selling considerably more than the term "butter" suggests. True, dairy products are at their best here, including the tastiest Cheddar in Hereford, but you can buy practically anything in the Butter Market from pets' toys to frilly underwear! On Wednesdays, Market Day, more flower, vegetable and fruit stalls appear. Going to market on a Wednesday remains a custom in many villages. I knew a farmer's wife from Fownhope who used to have a corner stall here for nearly sixty years. Nothing would

Sunday in High Town, feeding the pigeons

1670 ceiling in W.H. Smith's, High Town

Seventeenth century Merchant's House built into the facade of Littlewoods

prevent her going to market with her apples and flowers.

No-one can be expected to come out of the Butter Market into the pedestrian precinct of High Town with eyes glued to the pavement. However, it's only by looking down that you'll notice the contrasting paving stones. These slabs are the clue to the site of the Old Town Hall, demolished in 1862.

The twenty-seven oak pillars that supported the great timbered buildings are marked by darker paving stones. On this spot, Nelson received the Freedom of the City in 1802 in the ornate eighteenth-century Town Hall with its pretentious spire topped with dome-shaped bell tower.

Rows of timbered shops around the Town Hall, including the Old House in Butchers' Row would have created a claustrophobic impression, compared to to-day's open-plan precinct.

The Old House appears to be the only one left to tell the tale. Not so, for another seventeenth-century merchant's house can still be seen in High Town — less noticeable because it's above the eye-level and in an unlikely place. It peers, incongruously perhaps, from the first floor of Littlewoods!

Tucking the thirty-ton ancient house of Grocer Marchant into the facade of a department store, only a few yards from its original site, was no mean feat. One winter weekend in 1966, it was lifted on a massive timber chassis while engineers adjusted hydraulic rams in order to keep the house as perpendicular as possible.

Whether the ghost said to haunt the building withstood the experience, only time will tell! Less sightings have been reported since the move! Certainly his heavy footsteps tramping through the attics once terrified staff working late.

Who was he? The prime suspect is an apothecary who made a terrible mistake. Everyone knew Mr Stainsbury to be a caring chemist. One night, clasping his candle in one hand, he groped his way with the other along the interconnecting attics of the High Street until he reached his patient. The boy clutched his head in pain. Toothache or migraine was the cause. The chemist gave him something for it. In the dimlight he failed to check the substance: it was poison! The boy's death was agonising: his screams rent High Town.

The chemist paced the attics thereafter, reliving the shocking experience, finally sticking his candlestick into a beam to hold a noose. They found him hanging from a rope slippery with candle grease.

Years afterwards, apprentices took a grim delight in frightening those new to the trade by showing them the famous beam.

Entrance to the Butter Market beneath the clock tower

We're denied that dubious pleasure, but W.H.Smith have tried to make up for it. Their premises is acknowledged to be one of the most historic in High Town, although considerable alterations to the outside over the last three centuries belie the fact. Inside, a vast ceiling dating from 1670 has been exposed so that the customers can, by looking up, imagine themselves in a rich merchant's house in the seventeenth century.

Later, since the end of the nineteenth century, records show that both the premises now occupied by W. H. Smith were used as shops. It's difficult to imagine High Town without shops. They were preceded by the stalls of market traders. In the Middle Ages, crowds would have gathered, not only to shop but also to enjoy the public whippings. Indeed the brutal practice of watching victims whipped "until the blood came" continued till about 1830.

It was all part of the entertainment, together with bull-baiting, miracle plays, tournaments and Maypole dancing, which High Town offered as Hereford's social centre.

Pedestrianised in 1974, High Town has banished traffic and reverted to a more leisurely, social lifestyle. Never more so than in May, when the tradition of medieval Hereford combines with modern technology . . . and after opening the Fair, the Bishop hitches up his purple cassock to ride the dodgems. High Town, it appears, is still the place where it all happens!

12. Betrothal Chairs and Baby Cages in the Old House
(Map reference: 14)

Step into Hereford's Old House and you step into the seventeenth century. The family life of the period envelops you, yet the early history of the Old House itself is an enigma.

Apparently it was part of Butcher's Row. In a watercolour of l798, it appears to have joints of meat hanging in the downstairs window and possibly a customer standing in the door. 1621 is on the shields held by angels carved on the roof gables, presumably the date when the house was built. Above the porch is a shield of the Butchers' Guild of London. A ring which may have been used to tether animals for slaughter is also nearby.

By 1836 Thomas Wheeler, a saddler was occupying the house. He must have seen all the other houses in Butcher's Row demolished on the orders of the Improvement Commissioners . . . perhaps that's why he didn't stay long!

Certainly in 1840 John Roberts and a Mr Smith, also saddlers moved in,presumably with their respective families. They remained till 1872 when Mat Oatfield set up his hardware business here. For a short while the

Betrothal chairs of Holly and Ash, made by young men for their sweethearts

kitchen end was a wet fish shop, while the hardware trade continued round the other side.

It's not the customers that came and went, but an awareness of the families who used to live here that assail the visitor entering this dimly lit world of polished oak, candle wax and pot pourri.

Downstairs are the dining hall and kitchen. Imagine the family sitting at the table on wooden benches, with roast pig on pewter plates, cooked on the rotary spit in the kitchen. A cosy scene in winter, with the rushlights and candles and the fire flickering in the great stone fireplace, while they drank from pewter or horn mugs, replenished from the leather drinking jackets on the table.

And because this is Hereford, a royalist city, a toast to the king would be appropriate. The warming pan above the doorway to the kitchen echoes the sentiment "God save King Charles"! Surely the Master of the House must have been loyal to the King during the seige of Hereford in 1641?

Causes were won and lost here, that's certain. See the betrothal chairs in the kitchen, made of holly and ash by young men for their sweethearts. Apple or pearwood was also used to make cottage chairs for a couple's first home in Herefordshire.

Bedroom where the Master Butcher or Saddler and his wife would probably have slept

The Old House in High Town

The family would have sat upstairs during the evening, in the parlour or living room. In those days it would have had painted walls, tapestries, rugs and cushions. Here is the spinning wheel which might have occupied the daughter of the house while her betrothed made her chairs! The cast-iron fireback in the small fireplace maintains the royalist sympathies by bearing the coat of arms of Charles. On the ceiling are moulded fleur-de-lis and pieces of handblown glasses still remain in the windows.

Another flight of stairs leads to the second floor where four bedrooms interconnect which was very common in the seventeenth century. Bed curtains on the four-posters would have ensured privacy and also kept out draughts. The Master Butcher or Saddler and his wife would have slept on a rush mattress supported by ropes tied lengthwise and across. Pillows were the prerogative of the wealthy . . . and women about to give birth!

The smaller third bedroom may well have been used as a nursery. Here is a wooden swinging cradle. Toddlers are catered for too. Two late seventeenth century baby-walkers are surprisingly modern in concept. One is round, the other rectangular with a tray for toys. This design gives a child support while also giving it some freedom of movement.

The family would not have had the convenience of wardrobes and would have stored all their clothes in chests, most of which were fireproof and had secret locking systems. There were also dual-purpose chests with two drawers providing extra seating and storage space. Later, more drawers were added on top to increase storage space . . . and the chest of drawers was born! Look carefully and you can see where the two sections were joined!

The detail in the carpentry helps to bring the Old House to life. You can imagine the Master sitting in his special chair with indentations to accommodate his thumbs!

Less salubrious of course were the sleeping quarters of the servants or apprentices. It was upstairs in the attic for them! The glass panel in the ceiling of the smallest bedroom allows a glimpse into these uncomfortable quarters. It must have been unbearable in summer with ventilation limited by the small slits in the window panes.

Yet the aura of the house is distinctly happy. Its inhabitants and those who built it: carpenters, plasterers, glaziers, bricklayers and especially the woodcarvers, used their trades to enrich the city of Hereford.

The Old House still stands, appropriately, in the heart of the city. We cannot know how many daughters of this house took their first steps in a walking cage in its nursery and accepted betrothal chairs in its parlour . . . but the emotions experienced here are timeless.

The Old House is the family face of Hereford's past.

13. Footlight Fame for Hereford

(Map references: 17 & 10)

Hereford has the army to thank for David Garrick. His father, Lieutenant Garrick of the Dragoons was on one of his recruiting campaigns when David was born. Mrs. Garrick had left her two older children at home with their grandmother at Lichfield and accompanied her husband to Hereford.

And so, in 1716, the famous actor was born at the Angel Inn in Widemarsh Street. A plaque marks the place at the back of the Butter Market. Nine days later, he was christened at All Saints' Church, beneath the imposing crooked spire that, even in those days, was rumoured to be unsafe. Baby David's proud parents would have watched the Vicar baptise him in the 14th century font.

That was his first public appearance. The great Shakespearean actor became a master of performance both on and off the stage. He was a popular guest guaranteed to keep a room full of people entertained. Admittedly he was ostentatious but that was how leading eighteenth century actors were expected to behave. His fellow players were there to give him cues, keep out of his way and not distract the audience's attention during his speeches.

Perhaps it was his preoccupation with his own talent that prevented him recognising the rare promise in Mrs. Sarah Siddons, born in Brecon and with family connections in Hereford. The twenty-year-old actress made her debut at Drury Lane during the last year of Garrick's management, and he did not think well enough of her to advise his successor to re-engage her for the following season. She was later to win the appreciation of King George III — who did not care for Garrick's romantic style of acting!

For all his faults, Garrick's was a successful career of which Hereford can be proud — not least of the marriage that sustained him. Mrs Garrick's uncritical admiration soothed him after many a long, exasperating day at Drury Lane. In 30 years of married life they never spent a night apart. A poem published soon after their marriage, probably written by Garrick himself, sums up the woman who gave up her career as a dancer to identify with her husband in all that he did, attending rehearsals and charming his friends with her exquisite manners:

Who is the paragon, the marvellous she,
Has fixed a weathercock like thee?

A less successful theatrical marriage is described in "The Garrick Year", a novel by Margaret Drabble set in Hereford, his celebrated birthplace.

Statue of Nell Gwynne in the Coningsby Museum

Portrait of Bishop Beauclerk, Nell Gwynne's grandson, in the Bishop's Palace

Nell Gwynne's connection with Hereford, however has received much more attention than Garrick's. Oxford and London also claim she was born within their walls but antiquarians have made a convincing case for Hereford!

The exact date of her birth is indisputable. Her horoscope still exists in the Bodleian Library and the astrologer who cast it, followed the usual practice of inserting her birth-date in the centre of the map: 6 a.m. February 2nd, 1650.

Hereford records the place of her birth with a plaque in Gwynne Street which was originally Pipewell Lane, but renamed in Nell's honour. The original house was a mere hovel of brick and timber demolished in 1859 and all sources seem to agree that Nell was born in poor circumstances.

There were certainly numerous Gwynnes resident in Hereford in the seventeenth century but did they include Nell's parents? It's a fair assumption since her father was a Welshman.

An unprintable obscene poem of the period also points to Hereford as her birthplace. It describes her life as moving from "Hop Garden, Cellar, to the Throne." Hereford is, after all, the second largest hop-growing county in England!

And why did Charles II give Hereford Cathedral its organ? Many believe that this was his way of rewarding the city for giving him his Nell.

Font in All Saints' Church where David Garrick was baptised

Gwynne Street, West front of Hereford Cathedral in the background

Finally Hereford has the tacit agreement of a Bishop of Hereford to support its claim to Nell Gwynne. The Bishop was none other than Nell's own grandson, Lord James Beauclerk, the seventh son of the first Duke of St. Albans. When he became Bishop of Hereford in the eighteenth century, he refused to formally deny the legend of his grandmother's birth.

Bishop Beauclerk probably owed his name to Charles II's ingenuity. The king had to provide a suitable surname for his children by Nell. No doubt he had read in his history books that Henry I the father of more illegitimate children than any king except himself, was called Beauclerk because he could read!

Charles's grandson was certainly literate, but although he was Bishop of Hereford for forty years, he is remembered chiefly because in the last year of his episcopacy, 1786, the Cathedral's West Tower collapsed bringing down with it the roof and half the nave.

Beauclerk died the following year and was buried in the Choir near the Bishop's Throne. You can find his memorial in the Bishop's Cloister and his portrait hangs in the Bishop's Palace.

He survived Garrick by six years, by which time Nell Gwynne had become legendary, and Charles II's "Let not poor Nelly starve" had become a famous saying.

Although she was a notable actress, historians have only traced her appearance in about twenty plays. It wasn't her talent but her relationship with the King that immortalised the life of the girl Hereford claims to have been born in Gwynne Street. The cottage adjoined the boundary wall of the Bishop's Palace and was only a stone's throw from the Cathedral itself.

She could never have dreamt that one day her grandson would be the Bishop living in that palace and that a plaque would mark the site where her cottage once stood. The Future kept that secret from her in the same way as the Past refuses to verify her birthplace for us.

14. Beasts and Buried Treasure at the Library

(Map reference: 13)

Opposite the Close in Broad Street is Hereford's Cultural Trinity: Library, Museum and Art Gallery; three in one building. Also under the same roof is the Woolhope Room, home of Hereford's famous naturalist society, whose discoveries fill the Museum.

It's a convenient combination, facilitated by the size of the building. Nowadays though, the "Library", a term which, by popular usage, takes in the Museum and Art Gallery too, looks out of place in a street of lower buildings. This wasn't always so. When the Library was built in 1873, a three-storied Georgian house stood opposite, while next door was an equally tall Victorian villa. The Library's architect was therefore restricted to a smaller site. He could hardly have foreseen that the other houses would be demolished, leaving the Library towering above Broad Street in sole competition with the Cathedral.

Its huge pillars, ornate arches and heavily decorated window frames are, at first sight, pretentious. A second glance, however, takes in the intriguing sculpture. These carvings were, as the Hereford Journal reports, added in

Sculptured menagerie adorning the building

1874, "to suggest the purpose of the building, both as a museum, a library and a centre for Art and Science teaching." Science and Art are represented by finely modelled heads in medallions above the arcade which is supported by the four great pillars.

Below the medallions is a stone menagerie (see title page). Amphibians creep round the great arched doorway: water-shrew, beaver, walrus, hippopotamus, seal-elephant, rhinoceros, tapir, otter, sea-leopard and water-rat. There is also a "mullagong", though no-one seems to have heard of the species!

The creatures adorning the capitals of the four great pillars are more easily explained. Here are the squirrels of Europe, the monkeys of Asia and cockatoos, toucan and opossum of America.

The sculptors used the height of the building to advantage, creating a series of horizontal lines of carvings. One features the signs of the Zodiac. Above them come owls and animals of the chase: wildcat, fox, dog and rabbit. At either side of the facade, a larger animal head juts out. The peacock and eagle epitomise beauty and majesty, but why the seal? Apparently it represented the then Archdeacon of Hereford. He was Lord Saye and Seal. Doctor Bull, a former President of the Woolhope Club is there too. The Goat is the architect, Mr. Kempson, whose crest had a goat on it. Who is the monkey playing the cello? Perhaps it's a cheeky reference to the choirs of Worcester and Gloucester who join with Hereford to sing in the Three Choirs Festival?

The history of that festival is just one of the many fascinating local stories which can be unravelled in the Reference Library. The librarian on the enquiry desk is always willing to help if the sheer quantity of resources is overwhelming.

A splendid stock of local photographs, prints and old postcards are available, showing Hereford as it was. History suddenly becomes real. Hereford at the beginning of the twentieth century is recognisable but significantly different. Both horse and motor transport use the roads. In the villages, the portable cider press was a common sight, travelling from farm to farm, pressing the cider fruit so that local farmers could make their year's supply of cider. Then, as now, the River Wye in flood disrupted city life. In 1910, it swept over the Old Bridge, itself a favourite scene on many prints and old postcards. An equally popular subject was Hereford's annual May Fair which originated in the twelfth century. It started as a trading fair, but in the late 1880s, folk are pictured queueing up for the Great Lion Show, where according to the poster "the lady performs with forest-bred lions"! Showman Studt's " madcap machinery" was also drawing

Hereford's Library, Museum and Art Gallery in Broad Street

the crowds. They wanted to gallop on his "horse machine" and scream on his Mountain Climber switchback.

The bonus is that copyright on such photographs has expired, so you can photocopy them for a mere 10p in the Library! No wonder there's a market for nostalgia in the Local History department!

Before photographs, of course, prints provided insight into Old Hereford. Their accuracy varies, but together with old maps, they also help to form a picture of Hereford's past.

If the most fascinating part of the Library is the large Local History department, it's not the busiest. That accolade belongs to the Lending Library where ten tons of material are moved backwards and forwards every week by the staff. Indeed, Hereford's Library is probably the busiest in the West Midlands outside Birmingham, using just over 600,000 items a year. And that means the staff are coping with 11–12,000 items a week.

Upstairs the Museum offers a timeless retreat from all this activity. Here the History of Man in Herefordshire unfolds. On display are local flint arrowheads from the Stone Age.

The Iron Age Fort at Sutton Walls soon takes over the story. Spindle whirls and weaving combs are evidence of the textile industry that once existed there. A stone quern used for grinding corn for wheat cakes had an iron handle proving that iron was smelted at Sutton Walls.

The Romans left even more behind them in Herefordshire: brooches, javelins, spearheads, rings, bronze pins, Roman glassware and coin hoards. At Bishop's Wood over 18,000 coins were found. Such hoards reflect troubled times and the inadequacy of ancient banking. They represented a man's security and wealth. He buried them for safety in times of war and crisis, to be recovered when all was well again.

At Magna, near Kenchester more very valuable Roman finds were made: a tessellated floor, a builder's axe, building nails, painted wall plaster, decorated tiles . . . The list is endless.

Roman Hereford passes into Medieval Hereford with its city walls and plethora of Medieval treasures like the carved stone from St. Ethelbert's Well, spindle whirls and pilgrims' buckles.

Time passes. It may well run out allowing only a cursory glance at the Art exhibition, which changes regularly in the adjoining gallery.

No doubt about it — despite the convenient location and amalgamation of Hereford's Library with the Museum and Art Gallery, there's never enough time to see everything of interest!

15. Find the White Faces at the Cattle Market!
(Map reference: 18)

Hereford Cattle Market is second only to the Cathedral in attracting visitors to the city. Every Wednesday hundreds of daytrippers join farmers here for the sale of livestock.

Not for them are the soft toy Hereford bulls that peer from the windows of the city craft shops — they're here for the real thing!

Stories abound in Hereford pubs of promiscuous bulls earning their keep far beyond the old age of twelve. Formal burial of elderly bulls that have died of natural causes is by no means uncommon.

Revered as the world's main beef supplier, the Hereford is known for its ability to survive in severe winters as well as tropical heat. A record 27,000 guineas was paid for such an animal by a Canadian dealer in 1980.

Respect Hereford's cattle by all means — but be practical when visiting Hereford's Cattle Market! Canvas shoes are not suitable for picking your way across the manure-bespattered concrete!

The trail will lead you to the vast airy shed known as "The Langford Ring." It's a busy place; the pens are full of cows and weaned calves brought to be fattened for meat. The occasional cow will have a calf with her — the result of unsupervised mating. Thus, reprieved from "going for meat," she'll be waiting for somebody to buy her and "put another calf to her because she's got a good one there!"

The best part of going to the Market is chatting to the farmers. They're set to spend the day here buying and selling and are brimful of anecdotes which give local colour. They will invariably start the conversation, especially in the vast shed beyond the traders' stands, vying in broad Herefordshire dialect with the auctioneers' clattering echoes. While pigs are auctioned at one end and baby calves the other, it's worth scanning the latter for the characteristic face of the Hereford Bull.

The older farmers will tell you that Hereford used to be "the" beef for years before the continental cattle, the Limousin and Charolais came in, two years after "the war." Their growth was faster and their meat was leaner. However, cross breeding with Herefords ensures that the white face is still a familiar sight, here at the Market.

Those buying calves, however, are on the look-out for bright eyes and level backs. The criteria is that if you can get two or three fingers between a calf's shoulders, it's got room to fatten between them!

However, if you want the action, move on to the pig auction. The interest in pigs could well suggest that ham and bacon are more popular

Cattle for sale

Trader selling bath towels. "They'll fluff up when washed!"

these days than beef and lamb.

The old ewes are relegated to outside pens. Auctioneers in white coats strut around the raised platforms, peering into the pens and yelling out prices. When he yells "twenty-six fifty", for instance, bear in mind that it's per head, not per pen! The ewes are usually cheap (if you want one for the freezer!) but not "that" cheap!

If you're inclined to feel sorry for the ewes — sold off as "mutton" at seven years, you'll be told it's the humane way out, to prevent geriatric deterioration!

Next to the Langford Ring is a sight to distract you from the plight of the ewes. About seventy general merchandise stalls fill the area as far as the eye can see. Many of the traders have been coming to Hereford Market for at least twenty years, travelling from as far as Coventry for the event. It's hard to resist their convincing banter — and how cheap everything seems! Bath towels, you suddenly realise, "aren't meant to look wonderful until you wash them. As soon as you put them in water, they'll fluff up!"

The speed at which purchases are conducted is astonishing! These traders are professionals and courteous with it. There may not be changing rooms, but you'll be invited to try on a pair of jeans over a skirt, or offered a stool to make trying on shoes more comfortable.

Hereford Market is deservedly popular. The Welsh rate it highly, arriving in coaches every Wednesday for the excellent bargains to be had.

Certainly, a rare affability pervades the place. An indigenous characteristic? Could be, for aren't Hereford bulls unrivalled for their docility?

Penned sheep awaiting auction

Entrance to the Cider Museum

First type of Cider Mill, made of stone

16. The Spirit of the Apple
(Map reference: 22)

In the Autumn, a pungent smell of baking apples permeates the streets of Hereford. Appeased by these intoxicating fumes, motorists crawl behind pyramids of cider apples on tedious trailers. Driving becomes a time for reflection!

Why do we grow so many apples in Herefordshire? Why do we joke about cider smelling of overripe bananas?

Hereford's Cider Museum has all the answers! And so it should, for it is Britain's specialist Museum of Orcharding and Cidermaking. Situated next to Sainsbury's and opposite Bulmers, the Cider Museum is contained in a creeper-clad building, originally a cider-works but reminiscent of a barn with apple carts nestling in its outhouses.

Inside, the Cider Apple's Story through the ages unfolds. It starts in a painted orchard to the accompaniment of birdsong. Hereford's mild springs mean that frosts are unlikely to kill the blossom. We moan about our generous rainfall, but rain encourages the trees to grow, while our warm summers ripen the fruit.

Ripe cider apples, unlike eating apples, are very hard. That accounts for the mortar and pestle which early cider-makers used to break up the fruit by hand. Nearby is a hollowed out tree trunk, typical of those used to hold the broken fruit.

Then it's on to the first type of cider mill. Like those used to crush rock or mineral ores, it consisted of a circular stone trough in which one or more vertical stones were pulled around by a big horse. This process is shown on a press-button video. We see the cidermaker following his horse, knocking a few apples into the bed of the mill as he walks. Once the bed of the mill is covered, he throws several bucketfuls of water into the mill. The water helped to prevent the pulp from becoming too unmanageable and sticky.

Although these stone mills can't be mechanised, you will still see hundreds of them in Herefordshire. Local farmers were unwilling to adopt the mechanical rotary or scratter mill that replaced them.

A few, however, became travelling cider-makers like the one modelled in the Museum. They used a rotary mill mounted on a cart with a twin-screw press also on its own wheels hitched up behind the mill.

Once milled, the pulp had to be pressed. Wet, mushy apple pulp refused to stay in place so it was wrapped in straw. The stack of pulp and straw was called the cheese. Herefordshire cider-makers used horsehair cloths instead of straw.

In the Museum, the "cheese" has been built Herefordshire style. It looks like a giant eight-decker sandwich. The corners of the horseshair cloth are carefully folded to ensure no pulp is lost. A large heavy board is placed over the cheese to spread the weight and the press is gently lowered. The juice floods out into the large stone receptacle beneath.

Enormous wooden casks stand by, ready to receive the juice. Fermentation is exciting. Within a few days, the eagerly awaited froth appears at the bunghole. The juice is bubbling and is said to be "working" However, the cask must remain upright or the cider will go sour!

Fermentation used to be even more exciting because farmers had almost no control over it. Many tried to improve their cider by adding a hotchpotch of ingredients like beef steak, fatty bacon, rabbits' skins, beetroot and raisins. One story concerns a prize pig who disappeared during cider making one year. A year later its skeleton was found when a 400-gallon vat was cleaned out! "Best drop of cider we ever tasted," said the farmer! It's also suggested dead rats were thrown in for good measure, though these were probably uninvited guests!

Bacteria grew when air got into the cider. The result was a "mother". This definition caused hilarity amongst a coach load of Mothers' Union members! They had just discovered that a "mother" was a nasty jelly-like mass! It's the mother that causes cider to smell of ripe bananas, making it pour like syrup and giving it a slimy feel that turns it into a very unpleasant drink. What a relief to learn that modern ciders don't suffer from these disorders — due to better knowledge of ways to control fermentation!

Traditional farm cider was sugarless, very sharp and fairly strong. It was sometimes said to need two men to hold you down whilst you drank the so-called 'mixture of vinegar and water"!

Acquired taste or not, the Government chose to tax it. Cartoons capture the antics of the hated Excise men. Opposition to the tax became widespread and fierce in 1763, when for the first time government officials were given the right of access to private houses to search for cider. William Pitt is pictured opposing the Bill and asking, "Is an Englishman's home not his Castle?" Colliers in the Forest of Dean were said to have kidnapped an Excise man, threatening to keep him underground until the hated tax was repealed. It was abolished three years later.

Its abolition, however, coincided with the discovery that a fatal disease came and went with the amounts of cider made on farms each year. In the eighteenth century Endemial Colic was often fatal and was proved to be caused by lead poisoning from the linings of mills and presses. After that, cider was treated with suspicion for many years.

Potstill used in the seventeenth century to distill cider spirits

Looking at the pictures of the Bulmer family in the company boardroom, formerly Fred Bulmer's office

The revival of cider as a national drink began in 1887 when Henry Percival Bulmer, son of the Rector of Credenhill, began making cider from the fruit of his father's glebe in an old-fashioned stone mill of a neighbouring farm. He then moved his business into Hereford in partnership with his brother, Fred Bulmer.

The Cider Museum is constructed round Fred and Percy's original cider mill built in 1889. Fred Bulmer's private office which later became the company board room is preserved. Its walls are covered with photographs of the Bulmer family. Fred's initials., E. F. B. are carved into the panel over the fireplace with his brother's, H. P. B., and his father's, C. H. B.

Below the Bulmers' office are the Champagne Cellars, where the cider was made. Here are thousands of dusty green bottles stacked in racks. Giant oak vats big enough to hold a dozen people rule this musty underworld.

Upstairs in the King Offa Distillery are the French stills with which the Museum makes Hereford's Cider Brandy. The Museum staff do all the work involved including distillation, blending, bottling and labelling. Production began in 1984 after a 40-gallon copper potstill was imported from France.

Although similar to the French Calvados, this Brandy is essentially a product of Hereford cider, stored in barrels made from Hereford oak trees.

November 1992 saw the first batch of Cider Brandy that had matured for five years, released to the public at the Museum. It's ten times the concentration of cider. I can vouch for the lingering warmth of its flavour after attending a "tasting"! Gradually an increasing quantity of the five-year-old product will be available.

Distilled cider or cider spirit was once as popular as mead and sack in England in the sixteenth and seventeenth centuries, before it was taxed. On the Distillery walls are pictures of the Potstill used in the seventeenth century to distil cider spirits. It looks like an old-fashioned copper. Cider fed into it was heated by steam. The vapour passed through the condensing coil and the high-quality spirit was transferred to storage.

It has to be said, however, that the taste of Cider Brandy lingers for mere minutes . . . whereas a visit to Hereford's Cider Museum leaves a lasting memory of the ancient rural craft of cidermaking through the ages.

Corner of the Courtyard at Coningsby Hospital, showing two of the cottages

17. The Skeleton's Secret

(Map reference: 16)

You don't expect to find the prettiest historical site in Hereford opposite a D.I.Y. supermarket on busy Widemarsh Street. Neither do you expect to meet the uncompromising stare of a skeleton beneath a transparent floor!

Yet once through an oak door secreted in a protective grey brick wall, you enter a tranquil seventeenth century courtyard. The place is impenetrable. Traffic noise is banished as soon as the heavy door slams shut. Peace reigns. There's no room for the macabre here. For this is the historic Coningsby Hospital for "old soldiers, mariners or servingmen". It was founded by Sir Thomas Coningsby, the sixteenth century lord of the manor who wanted to protect and care for worn out soldiers and servants in a place where they could honour God.

What Sir Thomas created would be categorised today as sheltered housing, with nursing facilities available. He built twelve little cottages for his retired soldiers, using the stone from the derelict hostelry and Chapel of the Knights Hospitallers of St. John of Jerusalem which once stood here. Further building material was available from the neighbouring ruined monastic house of the Black Friars. This monastery, dissolved by Henry VIII, had conveniently become the property of Sir Thomas's wife, Philippa.

Her initial stands with Sir Thomas's over the fireplace in the dining room; The T.C.P. is often misinterpreted by visiting children as a well known pharmaceutical product! It can be pointed out that Sir Thomas, likewise did his best to take the sting out of poverty — if only for a few.

The monasteries had formerly offered shelter to the poor; the function and aim of Sir Thomas's Hospital was very similar.

He catered for the spiritual needs of his retired soldiers. He built them a chapel which opened on to a dining room which fed their bodily needs, while upstairs was an infirmary which provided care for the sick.

Dining Hall, Chapel and Infirmary are all interconnected. You can't stand in the Chapel beneath the trussed rafter roof, admiring the exquisite stained glass featuring the knights of St. John without being watched. A man in a white smock is peering at you from the Infirmary Balcony above. He is waiting for the service to begin. He will be able to follow it without even coming downstairs.

This realistic waxwork is one of many to be found upstairs in the Infirmary itself. Here a sick soldier is tenderly cared for by a woman whose job was to look after the pensioners. He lies on a straw mattress on a truckle bed. The sheet which covers him is handwoven and spun from flax grown in Herefordshire's Golden Valley.

In the opposite corner, a pensioner dozes at the table, with his hat over his eyes. He has apparently enjoyed his daily ration of beer, but his meal of bread and Shropshire cheese on a wooden platter remains untouched!

A Coningsby Pensioner from the twentieth century stands nearby, resplendent in his red uniform. His dress is similar to that of a Chelsea Pensioner. However, Coningsby Pensioners have first claim on this uniform, for Coningsby dates from about 1618 but Chelsea Hospital wasn't built until 1682. Indeed, many Herefordians believe that Chelsea Pensioners originated from those at Coningsby in Hereford!

The legend goes that Nell Gwynne, born in Hereford in 1650, was a frequent visitor to Coningsby Hospital and knew the inmates well. So she persuaded Charles II to found a similar hospital in Chelsea and to create the famous Chelsea Pensioners.

Locally, Sir Thomas's generosity and the requirements necessary to qualify for a cottage at Coningsby must have been well known. There were after all only ten cottages available, since Number 1 was occupied by the

The historic Coningsby Hospital in Widemarsh Street

Chapel from the Infirmary Balcony

Chaplain and Number 12 by the Corporal of Coningsby who was officially in charge of the others and responsible for their welfare.

Every week he gave each man "two loaves of bread made of good wheaten flour weighing 4lbs.", one on Monday morning and the other on Thursday. The barley malt beer ration was more generous! Two full quarts every day, one at eleven o'clock, the other at six o'clock at night.

Naturally there was no shortage of applicants for residence at Coningsby Hospital! Ex-military personnel had priority but occasionally a butler or valet who had served his master well for at least ten years, was allowed the privilege of a cottage. Mind you, there were rules to be observed: no haunting of "taverns or alehouses"! Public reprimands in the Hall by the Chaplain and the Corporal could precede expulsion for a third offence!

In any event, the skeleton staring up through a gap in the dining room floorboards was certainly no pensioner — either admonished or exemplary! The British Museum has assured us of that.

Who was he, then? His identity becomes a matter of urgency. Tile fragments of the thirteenth and fourteenth centuries were buried with him . . . So was he a Knight Hospitaller? Or a monk from Blackfriars Monastery?

The British Museum subscribe to the second view. Perhaps he was embarrassed by his deformed legs and was anxious to hide his twisted rickety limbs beneath a monk's robes? A recurring blood disorder or fever had also troubled him over the years. Determination and commitment to his calling might account for his withstanding painful attacks of osteo-arthritis, and surviving . . . probably until his fiftieth birthday.

His presence in the dining hall of Coningsby Hospital is strangely appropriate, for be he Knight Hospitaller or monk, his was a Christian lifestyle.

He worshipped in this place. And the worship goes on. "Can't you feel it?" asks the Museum Curator. "On the first Thursday of every month at 7 p.m., Holy Communion is celebrated here. Anyone can attend."

Through the wrought-iron gate off the Courtyard, the Monastery Ruins and 14th century Preaching Cross look on in silent approval.

Sir Thomas's instructions have been faithfully observed throughout the centuries. The cottages are still available for pensioners, but now there are only six. In 1958, each pair was converted into one and updated. They all have central heating and coloured bathroom suites these days! To qualify for residence at Coningsby Hospital, the husband must have been born locally, over 65 and have 4 years' military service to his credit. Sir Thomas's arrangements have stood the test of time.

As for the skeleton, he remains an enigma. But whoever he was, his spirit also permeates this place. Tranquillity reigns until the great oak door in the grey wall opens . . . and you step from the peaceful Past into the turbulent Present.

18. Elgar in Clover
(Map reference: 20)

Lord Mayor of Hereford was one title Edward Elgar didn't want! He was already famous when he moved to Hereford in 1904. Within four days of his arrival, he went to Buckingham Palace to receive his knighthood. Worcester gave him the freedom of the city. Hereford's leading citizens were equally anxious to honour the great composer. But how? Finally a deputation sped to his new home, Plas Gwyn on the corner of Vineyard Road and Hampton Dene Road — to ask him to become Mayor of Hereford!

The great man declined, but he appreciated the gesture and wrote his thanks. He would "never forget the touching way" in which the request that he should become Mayor of the city of his adoption was made.

An acceptable solution was found: Grocer Edwyn Gurney who had rented Plas Gwyn to Elgar, became Mayor — and Elgar was able to give himself to his music.

Plas Gwyn was just the place for him. The Mid-Victorian mansion enjoyed an uninterrupted view of the River Wye with the Black Mountains

Plas Gwyn on the corner of Vineyard Road and and Hampton Dene Road, where Elgar lived from 1904–12

in the distance. Its identity remains unimpaired to this day. Only the name has changed, to Elgar Court.

Elgar would sit at his upright piano which stood against the wall in his ground-floor study. Occasionally he would look out on to the veranda. Beyond, Hereford's gentle hills melted into the mystery of Wales. That combination prompted his Introduction and Allegro for Strings. He wrote, "Although there may be a little Welsh feeling in the one theme — to quote Shakespeare: 'all the waters in the Wye cannot wash the Welsh blood out of its body' — the work is really a tribute to that sweet borderland where I have made my home."

Just down the road from Plas Gwyn, the River Wye meets the River Lugg at Mordiford. It only took Elgar ten minutes to cycle to Mordiford Bridge. He was fond of fishing there. Indeed, written on the original score of "The Music Makers", which Elgar "sketched" around Mordiford, is "Four trout (decent), three (small) put back. Mr. D hooked salmon and lost it."

Fishing was one of his favourite hobbies. He would also walk along the river bank from Plas Gwyn and throw boomerangs down by the river! His wife, Alice, who inspired and admired his music, also shared his love of Nature. Her passion was birds. Their veranda became an open aviary, covered with honeysuckle and climbing roses where birds received their daily bread from the hand of Lady Alice. "Bung yirds", Sir Edward called the young birds — for he liked to play with sounds for fun!

A turtle dove joined the winged throng in 1909. The Elgars supplied it with a large wicker cage on the veranda. The cage door stayed open, to give "Dove" as they called her, complete freedom. Obviously they spoilt her. She wouldn't even make her own nest! So Elgar collected some hay, leaves and feathers for her and put them in the cage. Dove couldn't even be bothered to arrange the materials, she simply sat on them and laid an egg!

A part of the garden Dove would have been well advised to avoid was "The Ark". This was the outhouse which Elgar converted into a Chemistry laboratory. His explosive experiments weren't always successful! Nevertheless, he did patent a process for making sulphuretted hydrogen!

Guests were frequently entertained with stories of his experiments — notably the failures! Plas Gwyn was a great place for parties, but, in 1910, one party had to be relocated. Carice, the Elgars' only child, had developed Scarlet Fever during the Three Choirs Festival. Her father declared that the party must go ahead and promptly took over Harley House at the north-east corner of the Cathedral Close. He held his party there, issuing a joke programme for the 'Harleyford Music Festival'. It included some caustic comments on the Sewage Farm in his home parish of Tupsley, which suggests that the garden of Plas Gwyn didn't always smell of roses and jasmine — if the wind was in the wrong direction!

Just round the corner from Harley House, at 20 Church Street, lived Elgar's friend, Dr. George Sinclair, the Cathedral Organist. Until recently, a unique tombstone stood in the garden that of Dan, Sinclair's bulldog. The tombstone has now been temporarily removed. However, the new owner of 20 Church Street assures me it will soon be re-instated. After all, Dan is a local legend. He was the Organist's inseparable companion and had an ear for music. He sat under his master's platform when Sinclair was conducting during the Three Choir Rehearsals and growled when anyone sang out of tune!

Sinclair was keen on innovative new music, especially Elgar's. In 1928, he actually talked the Dean into allowing H.M.V. to record Elgar's works in the Cathedral using their mobile recording vans. When it was replayed, two Hereford ladies were heard chatting in a quiet part of the Dream of Gerontius! Elgar was understandably displeased. He probably didn't appreciate that broadcasting was in its infancy.

View of the Old Bridge from under the New Bridge

The Saracen's Head by the Old Bridge. A section of the River Wye near the Saracen's Head has been immortalised in Elgar's eleventh Enigma Variation

Sinclair and Elgar remained firm friends. Dan the Bulldog also made his mark on Elgar. The result: a section of the River Wye has been immortalised by a dog! Walk down Bridge Street and over the Medieval Bridge. Turn left immediately and stroll along the river bank past the Saracen's Head. Now pause, for here is the place portrayed in the eleventh Enigma Variation, under the heading G.R.S. (George Robertson Sinclair). Elgar tells us why:

"The first few bars were suggested by Dr. Sinclair's bulldog (Dan, a well-known character) falling down a steep bank into the River Wye (first bar), his paddling up stream to find a landing place (2nd and 3rd bars) and his rejoicing bark on landing (the second half of the 5th bar) G.R.S. said, "Set that to music!" I did . . . " !

The River flows on, affecting disinterest. On to Mordiford, along banks where Elgar walked, fished, meditated, — even threw boomerangs!

Up there, on the road which follows the river, stands Plas Gwyn where the summer of his genius blossomed.

He left Hereford for Hampstead in 1912. A friend assumed he was in clover in London.

"I don't now about the clover," Sir Edward Elgar grumbled, "I've left that behind in Hereford."

The Waterworks Museum, Broomy Hill

19. Water Works Wonders

(Map reference: 19)

A discreet lane off Broomy Hill leads down to one of the most fascinating places in Hereford. It's called "The Waterworks Museum", a name that fails to capture the exciting experience in store. For this museum, open on Sundays from 2–5pm, is unique and run by volunteers whose enthusiasm fires the place literally and metaphorically.

Through wide-open doors the heart of the Victorian Pumping station is visible. This is the 1856 Boiler House, the oldest part of the building. A volunteer energetically shovels coal into the blazing furnace. It's hard work and visitors are encouraged to take a turn!

The working pressure of the Boiler has been reduced because the engines are no longer pumping water all the way up to the Treatment Works on Broomy Hill; the modern waterworks has taken over. After a century's work, the Boiler has to be protected from undue stress! Its system has to warm up slowly so the fires have to be lit at least 36 hours before full pressure is required. The number of barrels of coal used is kept on a blackboard. Volunteers, who clearly love getting their hands dirty, come and feed it. Its appetite increases from one barrel on the Friday, to four on Saturday, until it's ready to devour a dozen barrels on the Open day itself! When the Boiler was first in use, the stoker was paid the equivalent of £1.55 a week and received no overtime pay when pumping continued beyond the specified twelve hours!

Hand-pumping, however, is the most popular pastime for visitors to the Museum. Few resist the invitation "to try the pump'! The earliest hand pumps were made of wood, still seen to-day on village greens. Even water-pipes were originally made of wood from tree trunks sliced and scooped, their two halves being replaced and fastened with wooden dowels or pegs.

Cast iron hand pumps eventually took over from wooden ones on village greens. The one in the Museum causes a lot of fun on Hereford's Regatta Days. Children are invited to "pump like this and get the river down! The more you pump, the more the river's going down — and all those chaps in boats will be rowing away and getting nowhere!"

Also pumping furiously away is the Hydraulic Ram. It spurts water out relentlessly, confirming that it needs no other form of energy to keep it going. Put it in a stream to utilise the energy and it will still keep a country house supplied with water. The reliability of these pumps is certainly impressive. The rotary pump has saved the face of modern technology on many occasions by clearing the bilges on yachts and ships during engine failure.

In spite of all the water about, it can still come as a surprise to learn that the deep well, visible under the floor, is connected to the River Wye. What is more, the level in the well tallies exactly with the level of the river. It's volatile, rising and falling accordingly.

Understandably the river level must not be allowed to drop below the level at which it's taken into the Waterworks.

To prevent this, gauges were used to register the river level. Many such gauges are displayed including a Teletalk phone which gives the reading when you lift the receiver. So, what happens if the river falls below the intake level? A steward is on hand with the answer, "You simply phone Harry up river and say, 'Harry, open it up!' and down comes a million gallons of water!"

It all seems too easy — like the effortless way the enormous Triple Expansion Engine turns its gigantic wheels. It's a monster breathing steam energy into usable power for pumping, making the atmosphere steamy with its sweat.

"The whole place is alive when this is going" says a steward, and proceeds to explain how this engine is "vertical, inverted, triple-expanding and condensing" — all at the same time! It's his pride and joy and no wonder; although phenomenally heavy, it's so delicately balanced that man-handling is no problem.

The author takes her turn at shovelling coal into the furnace at the Waterworks Museum

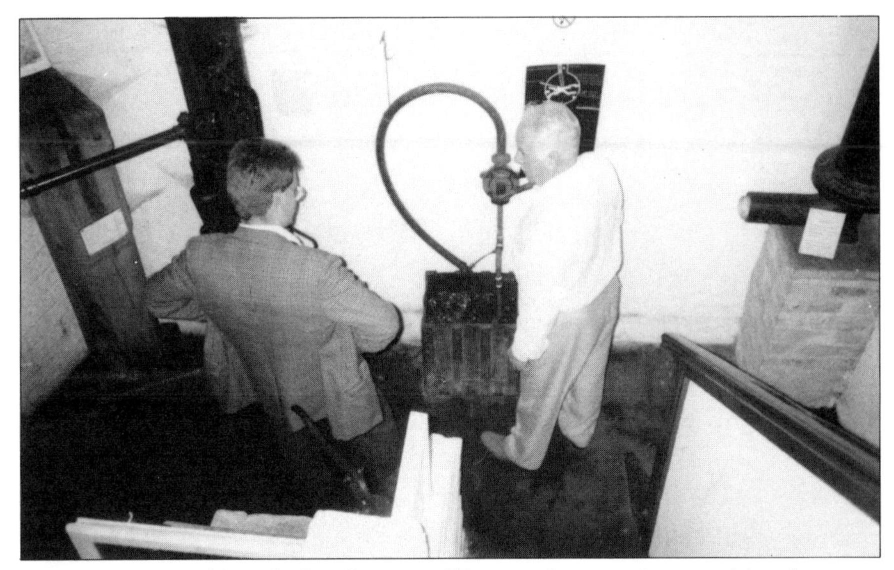

Visitors enjoy working the hand pumps. Here a volunteer shows a visitor how effective hand pumping can be

The affection the stewards have for the machines gives the museum the intimacy of a caring home. The visitor can't help responding to the warm welcome from Man and Machine, and leaves with the distinct impression that the engines at Broomy Hill are more valuable than the Mappa Mundi! It's certainly no surprise to learn that the Broomy Hill Waterworks Museum is reputed to be one of the best museums of its type in the country.

War Memorial outside St. Nicholas Church. Brian Hatton's name appears on the right of the base

20. Horses Hidden in the Hatton Gallery (Map reference: 21)

Hereford is possessive — almost secretive about Brian Hatton. Described by experts as a "genius, unique in the history of British art", the bulk of his work, nevertheless, remains in the Brian Hatton Gallery at Churchill Gardens, Hereford. His paintings and sketches exhibited there give a fascinating sight into the life of a brilliant artist, whose output, like Wilfred Owen's, was cut short by his tragic death in the First World War.

Brian lived with his parents and two sisters at "Mount Craig" on Broomy Hill, a stone-fronted mid-Victorian house with a big walled garden. His grandparents lived next door and his aunt just down the road. Their up-market properties are much the same to-day, climbing sedately up Broomy Hill to overlook the River Wye.

The three "Hatton" households would enjoy boating picnics together on the river and visit each other for afternoon tea and musical evenings. Brian, who was sitting in his pram sketching from the age of two, caused much comment with his preference for pencil and paper instead of toys.

The Herefordshire countryside with its cottages, fields, woods and long riverside walks inspired the young artist. Animals, people and movement were equally fascinating. He would sketch men and women working on their farms or gypsies selling pegs. Horses particularly intrigued him. The horse and cart delivering coal or garden manure would reappear within minutes on his sketch pad.

Love and understanding of horses is a Hatton characteristic. This passion, probably inherited from his great-uncle John Hatton, one of the founders of Hereford Race Course, is especially striking in Brian's equestrian portraits. His horses are individuals in their own right, like their riders.

Rural idyllic childhood could not last forever and Brian was sent away to school in Swansea, which he describes as being "so dusty and dirty and miserable after bright little Hereford." Nevertheless, he adapted to his new lifestyle in spite of not liking school much and missing his beloved Hereford.

Although dogged by ill health, asthma, bronchitis and, at sixteen, typhoid fever and peritonitis, Brian was resilient. His fighting spirit was evident at school where he hit "a beastly pugilistic fellow on the neck"!

His seventeenth summer was, however, spent quietly, recovering his strength and painting contentedly in Herefordshire. Meanwhile, his parents and Bishop Percival of Hereford discussed his further education.

The result was that, in January 1905, Brian went to stay with the Vicar of Ewyas Harold to be coached by him for Oxford University entrance. In this village only twelve miles from Hereford, Brian was able to escape from study to observe and draw country scenes. Some intriguing moments are captured in the sketches displayed in the Gallery. One features some tough-looking men who wanted to buy Brian's adopted stray dog, Spring, described as a "good rabbiter". Brian writes "The one with the mule wanted to buy Spring and then wanted to sell his own dog, which was the most remarkable freak I've ever seen, a sort of cross between a sheep dog and a wolf hound, with great bones sticking out of it." Another sketch shows Baptist Revivalists being baptised in the Dor Brook. Again Brian writes to his mother about it, "The poor beggars gasped, and could hardly walk up to the bank with their clothes all clinging to them, while one of the baptisers wiped the water out of their eyes with his smudgy hand, and the Baptists yelled 'Hallelujah!'"

Anatomy lectures at Oxford probably sharpened Brian's keen eye still further. They were actually meant for medical students, but Brian used the opportunity, as always, sprinkling the margins of his notebooks with sketches. During his time at Oxford he tended to gravitate to the familiar: the river where he could sketch in peace.

Mount Craig, formerly Brian Hatton's home on Broomy Hill

Painting portraits then took Brian to London to establish himself as an artist. In 1913 he went to Windsor Castle to draw Princess Alice's children — who misbehaved for him during the sitting! He was beginning to make his name by exhibiting at the Royal Academy, the Royal Portrait and other societies.

But then came the war. Brian was twenty-seven and had always had strong views on self-defence. At thirteen he had written "Even Ruskin says that fighting is essential, every nation who cannot fight goes to the bad and produces no great men or great things." So he enrolled at the Drill Hall in Hereford where he joined the Worcestershire Yeomanry as a trooper. It was a cavalry regiment, of course! Surprisingly he remained very fit, his concern being primarily for the horses. "It is getting so cold for the horses at night," he writes to his father.

His hasty marriage to Biddy (Lydia May Bidmead) by soldier's licence must have come as a shock to his family, who were informed by letter written on his one-day brief honeymoon!

Fortunately, he was stationed in King's Lynn for a year and so saw his baby daughter before he left to go overseas.

During the Egyptian campaign, Brian was reported missing. Shortly afterwards, an Australian corporal found "the body of a English Yeomanryman" in the desert. It was Brian, identifiable from the tiny photo of Biddy in his wallet, stuck on a postcard addressed to her.

Brian Hatton was killed on Easter Sunday, April 23rd 1916, at the age of twenty-eight. His name appears on the War Memorial outside St. Nicholas Church where Barton Road joins the Ring Road beside the New Bridge.

His pictures live on — in Hereford's Hatton Gallery. His identity is absorbed into the scenes he portrayed; farms, country folk and especially horses. He identified with horses as if he knew what they were thinking. His art has the power to let us into that secret.

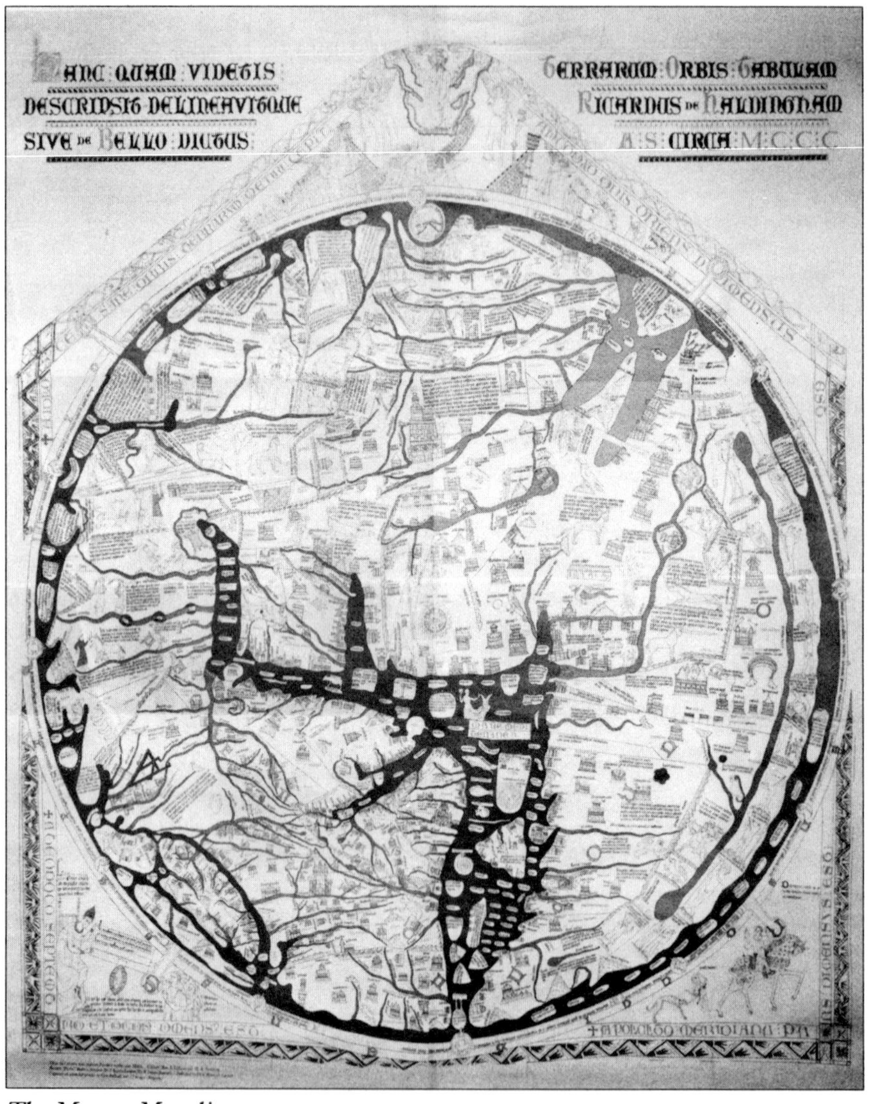

The Mappa Mundi

(Photograph by kind permission of the Dean and Chapter of Hereford Cathedral.)

21. Record Riches

(Map reference: Cathedral)

It's no secret that Hereford is the home of the only remaining complete Medieval world map: the Mappa Mundi. Something still remains for me to tell, however, which I believe will not be found elsewhere in the many publications which deal with the famous map.

In the early 1980s, it was still hanging relatively inconspicuously in a dark part of the Cathedral, next to the organ loft and opposite the Stanbury Chantry Chapel. At the time, I was teaching First Year Divinity at the Cathedral School and the map provided me with a valuable teaching aid, though I had no idea, then, how valuable it was. The best parts of the Old Testament were all vividly illustrated from the Garden of Eden to the Tower of Babel on this large piece of prepared calf-skin measuring 64" x 54". Inevitably Divinity turned into History and Geography. Such is the essence of the map.

Seven hundred years earlier, it had served a similar purpose — inspiring all who saw, read, or had it read to them with a hunger for knowledge. It was designed as an encyclopaedia for looking and learning, not for journeying. Nevertheless, there are 420 towns marked on it, suggesting the best stops on the way to the holy places of Europe. In Medieval England, maps were a luxury, sometimes used by nobles as a status symbol in the audience chamber, often bought by competing cathedrals either as an altar backcloth or to educate the congregation. To-day it's unique: an irreplaceable time capsule to the thirteenth century.

Medieval life was haunted by the all-important fact that it was man's last moments which mattered. Fearful paintings and carvings featured the sufferings of the damned and the joys of the faithful. Likewise on the Mappa Mundi, Christ sits in judgement above the world. On one side the Blessed are in Paradise, while on the other the Wicked are despatched to the literal "Jaws" of Hell.

At the top of the World is the earthly paradise of the Garden of Eden where Adam and Eve have already tasted the forbidden fruit.

The World's story unfolds as the mighty rivers of the Indus, Tigris and Nile flow south, and the Ganges east.

The Holy Land is in the middle of the map, with Jerusalem as the centre of the World. The Mediterranean Sea stretches beneath Jerusalem to the West; the scarlet Red Sea merges with the Indian Ocean. The British Isles is divided into Wales, England and Cornwall, with Scotland as an island. Hereford is marked, as is King Edward's brand new castle of Caernarvon.

Chained Library, Hereford Cathedral
(Photograph by kind permission of the Dean and Chapter of Hereford Cathedral.)

Meanwhile to the left of the Black Sea live the Essedenes who eat the flesh of their dead parents, and the grey-eyed race who see better by night than by day.

Marvels abound, from the gentle Sciapod sheltering from the sun under his foot to the people whose heads are in their shoulders — in unexplored Africa.

This was how the world was visualised two hundred years before Columbus discovered America.

Britain in 1289 is recreated in an explanatory film at the Mappa Mundi Exhibition. It was a colourful nation, noisy with the undisciplined energies of youth, characterised by tournaments, jesters, bawdy stories, minstrels, dancing and games including football which was already marred by hooliganism.

Hereford itself was busy with pilgrims visiting the shrine of Thomas Cantilupe, Hereford's Bishop who died in 1282. Miracle cures were associated with his remains: he was made a saint and his shrine in the North Transept still attracts visitors.

The man who created the Mappa Mundi, believed to be Richard de Bello who signed it, learnt about all the places he would never see from the many pilgrims visiting the Cantilupe shrine. Richard knew there were great continents and unknown civilisations to be discovered. For him the alligator and lion were as remote as the fabulous Hippopod with horse's feet and the jolly dragons in Ceylon.

In 1989, Moscow before Yeltsin seemed almost as remote to us! Yet it was from Moscow that an offer of help came when the news spread that Hereford Cathedral was about to sell the Mappa Mundi to pay for the vital restoration of the Cathedral itself. Alexei Petrov gave his stamp album to Hereford. It comprised a collection of over an hundred stamps from many countries, all showing a map of the country of issue.

Fortunately since then, the Hereford Mappa Trust, with the support of English Heritage has arranged for the Map to remain in Hereford.

A new centre is now being built in the south west corner of the Cathedral Close. This will provide facilities under one roof for the Mappa Mundi Exhibition and for the safe housing and display of the entire Chained Library.

The Chained Library is at present on view in the room over the South Transept in the Cathedral. However, the 1611 bookcase with its 1,500 chained volumes is only part of the whole collection of rare books. When the new centre is opened, the "whole" collection will be displayed in one place for the first time since 1842.

At last Hereford will be able to share the secrets of its Chained Library and its unique Mappa Mundi with the world.